Movement For The Actor

MOVEMENT

DRAMA BOOK SPECIALISTS

FOR THE ACTOR

Lucille S. Rubin
editor

(PUBLISHERS) • New York

Library of Congress Cataloging in Publication Data

Movement for the actor.

   1. Movement (Acting) I. Rubin, Lucille S.
PN2071.M6M6   792'.028   79–10461
ISBN 0–89676–010–3

10 9 8 7 6 5 4 3 2

Manufactured in the United States of America

Preface

FIVE OF THE SEVEN following articles grew out of a series of mini-articles which appeared in *Theatre News,* a publication of the American Theatre Association, from September 1975 through August 1976. Response to the series was enthusiastic but also indicated a need for further information in these specialized areas of movement. Accordingly, I asked my colleagues to expand and amplify their ideas, methods, and approaches. *Movement for the Actor* is the result of our joint efforts which, hopefully, will be of help to teachers, students, movement specialists, and actors.

Lucille S. Rubin, Editor
(V.P. Theatre Training UCTA•ATA)
Division of Theatre Arts
S.U.N.Y. at Purchase, N.Y.
February 17, 1978

Contents

AILEEN CROW *is director of her own School of Alexander Technique in New York City where she heads a teacher certification program. She served as Alexander coach for the American Shakespeare Festival in Stratford, Connecticut, taught movement for actors at the N.Y.U. School of the Arts Theatre Program, and was on the faculties of the Effort/Shape Certification Program of the Dance Notation Bureau and the Bank Street College of Education Summer Graduate School, New York City. Ms. Crow teaches at the American Dance Festival in North Carolina and leads groups in self-healing through breath, sound, touch, and movement and in touch for therapists. A former actress, she is a member of Healing Theater.*

The Alexander Technique as a Basic Approach to Theatrical Training

by Aileen Crow

THE ALEXANDER TECHNIQUE is a means of developing integration of the body and mind in action through the reeducation of kinesthetic perception. This process offers a positive experience of self—as light, expansive, flowing, and harmonious—leading to dynamic balance, coordination, and alignment. A pioneer in the field of mind/body integration, the Alexander Technique helps performers become attuned to themselves and others on a subtle yet highly energized level of organization.

1

F. Matthias Alexander, an actor who solved his own problem of repeated loss of voice, developed the Technique in the 1890s. His work attracted such students as John Dewey, George Bernard Shaw, and Aldous Huxley, as today it attracts many leading theatrical personalities. The Alexander Technique is recognized to be of particular value to performers and is taught in many acting companies, including the Juilliard School of Drama in New York City, the American Conservatory Theatre in San Francisco, and the former American Shakespeare Festival in Stratford, Connecticut.

One of the main goals in the physical training of performers is the integration of the mind/body, wherein the whole organism is in harmony with itself and ready for interaction. When performers can come to a "divine neutral"—a state in which the self is well balanced, flexible, and adaptable—they can become clear channels for the ideas they wish to express.

Effective training can begin when the student is able to assimilate technical skills without the interference of habitual faulty response patterns which distort mind/body harmony. This implies a certain level of awareness and control on the part of the student. The Alexander Technique provides a practical method for developing such awareness and control.

Posture, movement patterns, and breathing patterns express emotional and mental attitudes. Performers must be able to mirror, in movement and voice, many different personalities which change in various situations. If performers are "stuck" in habitual and characteristic tension patterns, they are limited in their ability to portray many characters and frequently may find themselves typecast. Through the Alexander Technique performers can release fixed tension patterns, leaving themselves open to assume many different body attitudes and breathing patterns, and to play those characters who are ecstatic, victimized, ingratiating, compassionate, "correct," or condescending. A choice can be made to select, perhaps, the "Macho" with a hard, fixed chest or the elated character with an open, free chest. These physical attitudes then become material for the creative process, to be worn by choice and with conscious skill.

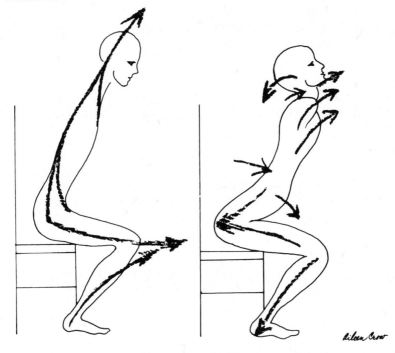

Getting up from chair

FIGURE 1. *Organized movement*

FIGURE 2. *Disorganized movement*

Tenseness (excessive muscular tension) is a common problem among performers. Energy that has become "stuck" does not flow freely within the body and therefore cannot freely flow out. Tenseness disturbs normal breathing, circulation, vibration, inner plasmatic flow, and contact with the environment. Balanced tension, on the other hand, is well distributed muscle tone and serves to keep the individual alert and ready for action.

Actors communicate with each other and with the audience by means of the ebb and flow of movement and breath. Performers whose flow is bound by tenseness and disturbed breathing patterns are likely to be out of contact with themselves, their fellow performers, and the audience. An audience responds empathetically to a performer: as he breathes, they breathe with him; if she sparkles, they feel delight. When performers experience themselves in their natural, expansive, and energized state, they are able to extend themselves to include their fellow players and the audience with ease.

Even performers who are directed to stand still on stage can be full of radiating inner movement once they realize that standing still need not mean assuming a rigid position and that relaxation need not mean passive sinking into gravity. Performers need to know how to be emotionally intense without straining physically, to be relaxed and at the same time energetically charged, and to have a clear focus on the acting task at hand without sacrificing their own personal well-being. To achieve these goals it is necessary to tune in specifically to the body's intelligence, to value it, and to listen to what it is saying. The body has a mind of its own and it is constantly giving us vital information—if we choose to receive it. With the Alexander Technique there is basic trust that this intelligence can be uncovered and developed, even when it has long been obscured by misuse, disuse, or miseducation. Students of the Alexander Technique make specific discoveries about what precisely they are doing which may be interfering with their natural ability to function well.

One example of interference is that of imposing on oneself an authority image of "correct posture." The military image (maintained by holding the chest up, pressing the shoulders back, and pulling the belly in) or the ballet image (which calls for an exaggerated lift of the sternum and depression of the shoulders) are but two examples of imposed body images. Such static holdings interfere with the free body movement and relaxed breathing the performer needs in everyday life and for the creative process. Rather than trying to live up to an image, one should tune in to the kinesthetic sense of the body as being in a dynamic balance. This requires a sensitivity similar to that needed for juggling rather than the use of muscular force to hold the "right" position.

One "authority" of 1907 indicated in his book, *Human Anatomy,* that men breathed abdominally while women breathed thoracically.[1] The fashions of the times supported this common nineteenth-century belief. The tight corsets and restrictive clothing worn by women at that time imposed control on the way they breathed and on the way they carried themselves. Just as fashions in clothing change, so fashions in posture and body attitude change, and both influence and reflect the body image. The Alexander Technique helps one find one's own unique way by uncovering one's own exquisite sense of balance, a balance that is waiting to be released and used.

Trying too hard, in the sense of using excessive and inappropriate amounts of muscular tension, is another common interference. Some people mistakenly believe that if their activities are not carried out with great intensity and force they are betraying inner weakness and helplessness. There is a tendency to confuse strength with strain and the result often causes physical damage. Students of the Alexander Technique discover there is indeed much work to be done, but it is "effortless effort." Concentration on the process and on avoiding interferences replaces getting a result by "muscling" it. Flexible strength can develop when the emphasis is placed on economy and ease.

Interference caused by excessive involvement frequently can be seen in the common response to the direction "take a deep breath." All of us have learned to haul up our chests with great effort, believing we are filling our lungs. The easier and more efficient way is to exhale, releasing present air, and then to allow air to flow in as the result of changes in air pressure within the lungs. F. Matthias Alexander, who was called "the

Breathing Man'' of the early 1900s, noted that it was "not necessary even to think of taking a breath,'' and his students were guided to detect and inhibit any psychophysical stress or strain.[2] Carl Stough, a present day teacher of the science of breathing coordination, informs us that forcing can "destroy the natural breathing pattern, alter the position of the chest and weaken the muscles of breathing.''[3]

Proper body alignment and relaxed breathing are inseparable. Interference with reflex breathing is expressed physically in four general ways:

1. The lower back ribs may be compressed, holding the back arched in such a way that rib expansion on inhalation is restricted;
2. There may be an increased sternal angle, a result of lifting the chest to inhale;
3. The muscles of the neck and the upper trapezius and pectoral muscles may shorten as the result of unnecessarily involving them in inhalation;
4. The lower front ribs may be flared as a result of conflict between the intercostal muscles and the action of the diaphragm.

Interferences with breathing are experienced as discomfort, pressure, strain, or pain. The Alexander Technique, by teaching students to recognize and release unnecessary tensions and superfluous muscular effort in activities, facilitates effortless deep breathing and vocal production.

Discomfort is a signal of physical, mental, or emotional imbalance. Mental and emotional distress have their physical counterparts. Bjorn Christiansen points out that particular disturbed breathing patterns accompany specific psychological problems.[4] Just as breathing is improved when problems are resolved, problems can dissolve when the breathing is freed. Physical and emotional well-being, then, serve the performer as a referent. Performers can then take on other people's patterns and still maintain their own well-being within themselves or be able to regain quickly their own organized patterns once "out of character."

F. Matthias Alexander himself suffered from repeated loss of his voice in performance. Neither rest nor doctors could help him; consequently, he undertook a long project of self observation using three-way mirrors. He discovered that in anticipation of speaking he was pressing his head back and down, sucking in breath, depressing his larynx, lifting his chest, and compressing his spine. (This is a typical picture of respiratory difficulty.) Along with excessive muscular tension throughout his body, these elements constituted distortion of his entire physical–mental mechanism. He also discovered that his feelings were unreliable as a guide, for what felt natural to him was his habitual faulty response pattern. He learned to inhibit his stressful response when he felt the impulse to speak and to give himself time to direct his actions in an organized way by concentrating on the "means whereby," instead of "end gaining." In today's terminology this means he became more process than result or goal oriented; he began to live in the moment, the here and now, rather than pushing to gain a goal "by hook or by crook."

Alexander also discovered what he believed to be a "primary control" over interferences. Frank Pierce Jones, the late Alexander researcher, articulated his understanding of Alexander's principles of primary control in the following way:

1. The reflex response of the organism to gravity is a fundamental feedback mechanism which integrates the other reflex systems.

2. Under civilized conditions this mechanism is commonly interfered with by habitual, learned responses which disturb the tonic relation between head, neck, and trunk.

3. When this interference is perceived kinesthetically, it can be inhibited. By this means the antigravity response is facilitated and its integrative effect on the organism is restored.[5]

Students of the Alexander Technique learn to observe themselves in action and to become aware of their particular tension patterns. They consider questions such as: what do you do to prepare for action? do you get ready to move or speak by tightening? how is your weight distributed? do you expect movement to be difficult or do you expect it to be pleasurable? do you hold your breath in order to concentrate? do you tense neck muscles in order to move your hands? are you compressing yourself or giving all your body parts enough room? Of course, what happens on the physical level reflects one's mental and emotional functioning.

Teachers of the Alexander Technique are trained to sense potential movement in the student's body and, through touch, to encourage the movement of energy through previously immobilized parts. Freely flowing energy facilitates a redistribution of body weight and a profound sense of the relationship between body parts. Neither the Alexander teacher nor student uses any muscular force in allowing new energy patterns to develop. Alexander teachers use an extremely light and delicate touch and are sensitive to the student's energy distribution and balance in motion. At the same time, the teacher's own balance and energy flow is crucial to his or her perception of the student.

Students are guided to understand kinesthetically the following general directions for sound anatomical usage:

Neck Free

Eliminate any superfluous activity of the neck and upper trapezius muscles during movement of the limbs or other body parts. Do no unnecessary work to maintain the head in a fixed "correct" position. The neck is relaxed in breathing and speaking.

The Head in Delicate Balance Atop a Lengthening Flexible Spine

Float the head up off the end of the spine as though the head were extending out into space. The head–spine relationship is crucial to the Technique. Downward pressure of the skull on the spine exaggerates the natural curve of the spine, contributing to lordosis, kyphosis, or scoliosis. The weight of the head sagging or pressing down on the spine encourages a pattern of compression for the whole body. As the Alexander teacher guides the student's head into equilibrium, the spine can lengthen in both headward and tailward directions. This release of the spine expands the middle back, helping the lower back ribs to spread on inhalation. It also allows the "tail" to drop, eliminating any need to "tuck under," as the pelvis is now free to balance atop the legs rather than be held in a static position.

Lengthening the spine is not the same as holding it straight. Holding the back flat or the spine straight reduces flexibility. The spine can lengthen while it is curving and twisting because the vertebrae are being afforded more space in which to separate.

The Torso Lengthening and Widening and Filling Out in Depth

Think of the torso (rib cage and pelvis) as a cylinder which can be shaped in many ways without shrinking any part. Each part of the torso adjusts to and contributes to the shaping rather than some parts overworking for others that are inert or inflexible. As Raymond Dart has shown, the musculature can be understood as double spirals wrapping around a flexible central axis.[6]

Shoulders Out

Widen across the chest front and back. Expansion of the front need not be at the expense of compressing the back, and opening the back does not mean that the shoulders move forward to become a heavy weight on a narrowed front. Cultivate spreading; release into expansion. Visualize space at the shoulder joints and an outward energy flow from the center of the chest out through the fingertips. This sense of flexible width can be active even as the upper back twists in walking.

Hip Joints Free

The torso, particularly the pelvis, balances on the flexible rotary thigh sockets. Clear use of these largest joints of the body is essential in the prevention of back problems and to economical everday use of the body. Problems arise when the lower back is used as the main hinge in bending, instead of the hip joints, or when the hip joints are used only as hinges instead of allowing the rotary action of these ball and socket joints. In walking there is a slight backward–forward swing of the pelvis as the legs swing through. Holding the pelvis in a fixed position, even a "perfect" one, can be a source of back trouble.

Locked knees (legs that are hyperextended and inwardly rotated) tilt the top of the pelvis forward, prevent the poise of the pelvis atop the legs, and cause compensating lower back compression. Also, hyperextension shifts the body weight onto the insides of the feet, contributing to collapsed arches. The release of the knees is accompanied by a slight outward rotation of the legs at the hip joints which centers the balance of the pelvis over the hip joints. The foot and knee should each point in the same direction when the leg is bearing weight.

Knees Away From the Torso

Decompress the hip joints by directing the legs away from the torso instead of pulling them up into it. The body, responsive to directive thought, has the ability to condense and to expand.

The directives outlined above apply to the most common problems and may be modified or changed in particular instances. For example, there are some people who are "scattered" and may need to "pull themselves together," but most people need to allow themselves more space. Stress leads to contraction, pleasure to expansion. The Alexander Technique leads to a dynamic balance, away from the extremes of rigidity or limpness—both of which are symptoms of stress.

Emotional factors enter into the process of change. To alter one's equilibrium is to change one's state of consciousness, body attitude, and self image. When movement and breathing patterns change through Alexander training, emotional and mental states may also change. For example, one actress realized that she had been accepting the tenseness in her back and neck as the price she had to pay for success in her career, while an actor found that he had been restricting the rotation of his hip joints for fear of being a "swivel hip."

Many students realize that they have accepted negative images of themselves, such as being clumsy, uncoordinated, or unattractive. Students of the Alexander Technique find that their self images greatly improve and that a positive sense of self is fostered by a harmoniously organized body. More than one student has been transformed from an "awkward klutz" to a graceful mover.

The Alexander Technique is taught by the instructor guiding the student through movement using such everyday actions as sitting, walking, writing, and reaching, as well as singing, playing an instrument, ballet barre, T'ai Chi, eye–hand coordination games, balancing games, and physical exercise.

A skeleton is used to provide a clear understanding of the articulation of body parts. The mental image a student has of a body part structure determines how that part will be used. For example, if the occipital joint is clearly visualized, the poise of the head on the spine will be easier to find than if the student thinks of the neck and head as one unit or thinks of the neck as extending only as high as chin level. It is not uncommon for new students to be unaware of the location of their hip joints and shoulder joints. Their body use changes for the better with a clearer understanding of structure.

From the beginning of the Alexander Technique training,

actors learn to sense and direct their own energy without removing themselves from their surroundings. Energy flowing through and radiating from the body connects inner sensation with outer spatial awareness. Simultaneous inner and outer awareness aids projection on stage while keeping performers in good touch with their own well-being under the stress of performance.

After repeated guided kinesthetic experiences, students of the Alexander Technique come to sense their former static tensions as uncomfortable and alien. A sense of self as a pleasurable, integrated totality develops, which helps the performer to open the mind/body to the creative process of acting.

FOOTNOTES

[1] G. Piersol, *Human Anatomy* (Philadelphia: Lippincott, 1907), p. 168.

[2] F. Matthias Alexander, *Constructive Conscious Control of the Individual* (New York: Dutton, 1923), p. 201.

[3] Carl Stough, *Dr. Breath* (New York: Morrow, 1970), p. 205.

[4] Bjorn Christiansen, *Thus Speaks the Body* (New York: Arno Press, 1972), pp. 44–52.

[5] Frank Pierce Jones, *Body Awareness in Action* (New York: Schocken, 1976), p. 151.

[6] Raymond Dart, "Voluntary Musculature in the Human Body, The Double Spiral Arrangement," *The British Journal of Physical Medicine* (December 1950).

JENNIFER MARTIN *holds a Ph.D. from the University of Michigan where she headed the stage movement training program. Currently, she is on the faculty of the theatre and dance programs at the University of Iowa as stage movement coach and choreographer. Her work as a guest choreographer ranges from concert dance to dramatic choreography in educational, community, and commercial theatres.*

Successional Flow: An Approach to the Integration of Stage Movement Training

by Jennifer Martin

VIEWED IN THE CONTEXT of a theatrical tradition which extends back to the Greeks, movement training for the actor is a fairly recent development. While the shaping of an actor's physical capabilities has been attempted to varying degrees throughout theatrical history, attempts to systematize movement training for the actor have been largely confined to the last one hundred years.

As actors responded to their audiences' changing tastes in

performance styles, physical aspects of their own performance changed accordingly. Theories of acting were not concerned with the specifics of movement training, and it was not until the time of François Delsarte that a system of movement training was recognized.

During the mid-nineteenth century, Delsarte engaged in an extensive study of human movement. From detailed records of his observations he formulated laws of movement and expression that were brought to the United States by Steele MacKaye, who popularized Delsarte's principles. Because Delsarte's laws of movement were appropriate to acting styles in the United States, aspects of Delsarte's laws were systematized and widely taught during the early years of the twentieth century. Because it was used by those whose understanding was incomplete, however, the "Delsarte system" fell into disrepute.

Since Delsarte's time there have been numerous theories and systems of actor training and more highly specialized theories of movement training. With new approaches to actor training have come new approaches to stage movement training which attempt to prepare the actor for the physical demands of new performance situations.

The purpose of this discussion is neither to evaluate movement training as it has existed nor to add yet another system to those already existing. It is, rather, to propose a means of integrating the many specialized areas of movement training for the actor through a principle first described by François Delsarte—successional movement.

A successional movement flows through the body joint by joint. For example, landing from a jump is not a straight-legged, flat-footed movement but rather a sequential flow of movement through the toes, foot, ankle, knee, and hip. An embrace may begin in the chest and flow through the shoulder, elbow, hand, and fingers as the arms are wrapped around the body of another person. The successional flow can be in any direction—inward, outward, headward, or footward. The point is not to omit any part of the body.

In the midst of the current trend toward greater specialization, the concept of successional movement provides an
overview of the many technical skills an actor is expected to
possess. The use of succession is common to such varied activities as thrusting a foil, performing a bow or curtsey,
executing a mime walk, and falling down a flight of stairs.
Seldom is the relationship between these activities explored,
and as a result they remain specific skills to be employed when
needed rather than serving as part of an integrated movement
training program.

Increased specialization has brought with it an increasing
number of specialists who are eager to teach. Actors now have
the opportunity to study historical dance with a period
movement specialist, mime with a mime, circus technique from
a clown, and so on. The list is growing longer every day. The
problem, however, is not so much an overabundance of
specialists as finding a way of unifying the somewhat isolated
technical specialties into a coherent and useful training experience.

The methods used to teach stage falls and rolls will illustrate
the problem. Dance techniques and martial arts as well as
gymnastics generally prescribe falls and rolls which are
dependent on or at least related to specific movements (e.g., a
forward roll out of a head stand). In order to make such specific
falls and rolls useful to the actor, the movement must first be
adapted to the actor's physical ability to execute the particular
skill and then to the situation and stage setting. Beginning with
the sequential flow of the actor's body and allowing that flow to
be governed by the situation can eliminate the additional step
of learning a skill that must then be adjusted. Because the
movement originated within the actor as a response to the
action of the scene, the stilted quality often resulting from
copied movement or movement learned as an isolated skill is
avoided.

Unlike many set skills, the concept of succession is sufficiently flexible to be applied to any context or stage con-
figuration. When a fall off a platform or down a flight of stairs

is required, it is unlikely that falls and rolls from a set discipline would suffice. Again, the technical skill once learned on a flat surface would need to be adjusted to a surface with several levels. Too often a set skill is applied to the needs of the situation without sufficient consideration of the context in which it is used and the facility of the body executing the required action. Many actors experience a fear of falling which is intensified in rehearsal and performance situations. Apprehension leads to muscular tension and, consequently, to an increase in the likelihood of injury. Placing the emphasis on the motivation in the specific setting will direct the actor toward a natural joint by joint response and, with practice, a gain in confidence. In time the actor may even choose to expand his facilities through other disciplines such as dance, gymnastics, and the martial arts.

The principle of succession is illustrated, in elementary form, by the photograph of a front fall from the knees (Figure 1). It is the very same principle shown in the more complex side fall and roll from a platform (Figure 2). The successional flow of weight through the fingers, hands, wrists, elbows, and shoulders in the front knee fall is analogous to the successional flow through the toes, foot, ankle, knee, and hip of the side fall. In these two falls it is not so much a question of executing a particular set of movements but of completing the movement in a successional flow. In the follow-through of the roll from the side fall, the principle of succession continues. Contact with the floor flows across the back, through the hip, thigh, calf, and finally to the foot of the extended leg.

In stage fighting classes I teach falls and rolls (including those pictured here) without mats or protective floor covering of any kind. The use of successions has made such accommodation unnecessary. Working on a bare floor has the additional advantage of direct transfer to the performance situation. For

FIGURE 1. *Front fall from the knees*

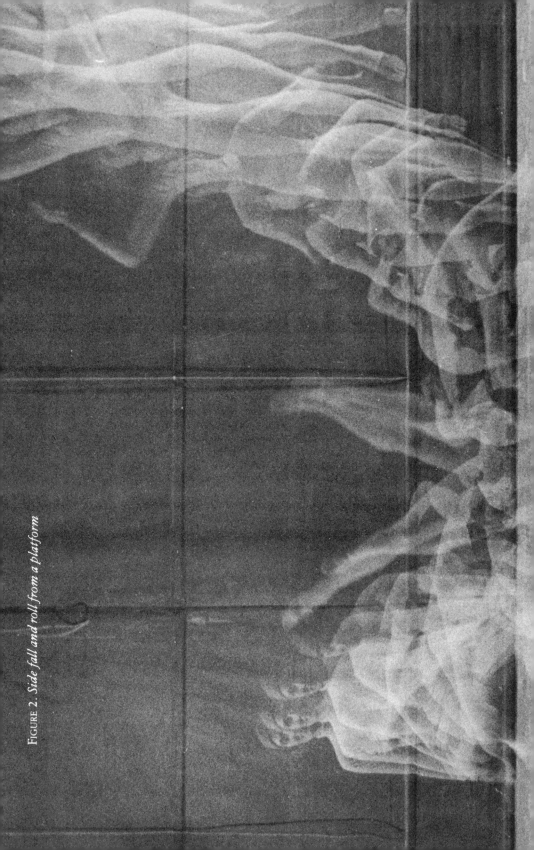

FIGURE 2. *Side fall and roll from a platform*

actors who become accustomed to working on mats, the transition from a padded to an unpadded surface is a time-consuming adjustment that is not needed if successions are first learned on a wooden surface.

The successional approach to stage combat is not meant to replace the disciplines from which actors have borrowed techniques of falling, rolling, punching, slapping, and all the other aspects of stage fighting. It will, however, provide a base upon which all such skills may be integrated. Learning a new fall then becomes not just another skill but rather a new application of a basic principle of human movement.

The use of succession in stage combat may easily be extended into mime, dance, and other aspects of an actor's movement technique. For example, the mime walk may be regarded as a series of successional movements. As one foot is placed on the floor, the other foot begins a successional roll-through from the heel through the foot to the toes. The chest, shoulder, and arm isolations that are used to create the illusion of pulling or pushing are inward and outward successions respectively.

Similarly, in dance a *grand plié* followed by a *relevé* is a footward then a headward successional flow of movement through the legs and feet. The examples are as numerous as the movements themselves.

Stage combat, mime, dance, and other movement techniques may be approached in many ways, and there are well-qualified specialists who offer excellent training. If all these valuable experiences are to provide a well-rounded movement proficiency, however, specialized techniques must not remain isolated skills; they must become prat of a larger movement vocabulary. Successional movement provides an overview. Of course there will be isolated circumstances where successional movement is not viable, but in general the concept of succession provides a means of integrating the varied aspects of the actor's movement training.

Another aspect of stage movement training is the development of an actor's physical facility. This includes such things as strength, flexibility, endurance, balance, and coordination. Physical facility cannot be separated from technical skill, and, indeed, improvement in one area feeds the other. For various reasons, however, some training programs treat facility and skill as two separate entities. Although preparatory exercises from gymnastics, dance, the Eastern martial and meditative arts, and body mechanics have traditionally formed the basis of the actor's exercise program, a number of self-use systems have recently provided new ways of realizing physical potential. The content and approaches of both traditional and self-use systems vary widely, and although their common objective is to maximize the actor's movement capabilities while minimizing tension, the end result as well as the method of achieving that result differ considerably.

Again, the purpose here is not to offer an alternative to approaches that have been successful in the past, but to suggest a new perspective. Except for those who are strict adherents to a particular system, the approach generally taken to stage movement training is an eclectic one. Breathing and relaxation exercises from yoga are combined with hamstring stretches from the Nikolais dance technique, Grotowski's early version of the cat for arm and shoulder strength, and the gymnastic V–sit exercises for balance. The combinations are infinite. Regardless of the origin of any exercise, its effectiveness is dependent in part on the actor's understanding of how that exercise relates to his body, and this is where successions are valuable.

For example, sit-ups—or abdominal curls as they are sometimes called—are part of most training programs. There are many variations, but the basic pattern involves a curling of the torso in which the head is brought toward the knees. Too often this exercise remains merely an action which with repetition will improve abdominal strength. The "plow," which is designed to improve back and leg flexibility, begins in a supine position as does the sit-up. However, the curling motion of the plow begins at the other end of the torso so that the legs are lifted over the supporting shoulders and the feet come to rest on the floor beyond the head. While the function of the plow exercise is quite different from that of sit-ups, the successional flow of movement is very similar. Both use a successional flow through the joints of the spine; they just begin at opposite ends.

While actors are generally aware of the differing purposes of the sit-up and the plow, few realize the relationship of these movements. Both are spinal successions. The exercises are too often understood only in isolation and not in the larger context of human movement. The same succession has many other applications, but one additional example will suffice to make the point.

Many of the voice and movement classes I have observed were begun with a ''round-over'' of the torso into a standing ''low hang.'' Teachers stressed the sequential flow of movement through the spine beginning with the rounding forward of the head. With various images they guided the actors to a release of tension. The common spinal succession is obvious, but the ending position of the standing round-over, the plow, and the sit-up is also similar except that the weight of the body is supported on different bases: for the round-over, on the feet; for the plow, on the shoulders; and for the sit-up, mainly on the hips. While the round-over's immediate function is generally understood, little or no attempt is ever made to relate it to a larger context.

Because my orientation to the development of physical facility is with a strong emphasis on anatomical alignment, my use of successions as a way of relating the various aspects of movement training may be predictable. The spine is central, and successions are easily defined in movements of the spine.

As in the area of technical skill, there are some exercises in physical facility which are not easily related to the concept of succession. Where no useful relationship exists, none should be forced. However, where a relationship does exist, successions not only provide a means for integration of physical facility and technical skill within their respective parameters, but also for integration of both areas of training into a useful whole. Increased back flexibility from the plow is related to the backward roll, which has become easier to execute as a result of improved flexibility. Physical facility and technical skill are no longer two separate areas of stage movement training but application of the same successions to different needs.

The final application of succession—to physical characterization and dramatically motivated action—may be more closely related to the work of an acting coach than to that of a stage movement coach. However, because I am committed to the relationship of all aspects of the actor's physical communication, it is included here. To provide a background for this view of successions it is necessary to return to Francois Delsarte.

One caution must be extended before outlining Delsarte's basic principles. Because he used drawings to illustrate his findings, only one instant of the movement could be captured. Unfortunately, actors began to copy poses they perceived in the drawings in order to indicate emotion or states of being. The result was stilted mimicry, and the Delsarte system was held responsible for the "bad acting" that resulted. The problem lay not in Delsarte's findings but in the interpretation and use of those findings. Some of Delsarte's concepts are now dated, but his basic principles of movement remain useful guides. The important point is to use them as guides and not as absolutes that require slavish adherence.

Successions are contained in Delsarte's three Orders of Movement. Regarding succession as the greatest order of movement for expressing emotion, Delsarte defined two categories. True successions, he noted, expressing the good, true, and beautiful, begin at a center and flow outward or start at the head and flow footward. Reverse successions, expressing evil, falsity, and insincerity, begin at an extremity and flow inward or at the feet and flow headward.

To illustrate this principle quite simply, place your hand in front of you, fingers extended and palms up. Imagine a small pea in the center of your palm. Beginning with the tips of your fingers, close your hand around the pea. Repeat the closing several times, and remember that it is the flow of movement and not the final position that is important.

When you have the feeling of an inward succession, try an outward succession. The starting position is the same: hand open, fingers extended, palm up. Imagine a pea in the center of your palm. This time begin closing the palm around the pea and work out to the tips of the fingers joint by joint. The ending position of the hand will be different from that of the inward succession, but, again, focus your attention on the flow of the movement and not on position. Repeat this closing several times.

When you have a clear sense of the flow of each succession, alternate the two. If you have differing reactions, try to determine what they are as you compare the two successions. According to Delsarte, the first succession, because it begins in the extremity and flows inward, is a reverse succession and has connotations of evil, falsity, or insincerity. The second, because it begins in the center and flows outward, is a true succession which expresses goodness, truth, or beauty.

Because Delsarte's observations were based on perceptions rather than on some measure of motivation, it is important to put your reactions into that context as well. For example, many actors with whom I have worked experienced different responses to the successions while they were executing them in contrast to while they were observing them. The usual response is that the true or center–outward successional flow is not a familiar movement. This explains why so many actors have a negative kinesthetic response to it. Yet when those same actors see the true succession executed by someone else, their reaction is a positive one usually expressed in such terms as "protective," "nurturing," and "gentle."

Aside from successional flow, there are other features of movement which determine how any given movement will be perceived. For example, the amount of tension which is applied and the speed at which the succession is executed may both contribute to meaning. If the true succession as Delsarte defined it is accepted as having positive connotations, those positive qualities may be emphasized with minimal use of tension and a slow flow of movement. If on the other hand the amount of tension is markedly increased (the flow and the movement remaining the same), the movement may acquire negative rather than positive connotations. In utilizing Delsarte's concept of succession, then, it is important to consider it as one of several properties which contribute to the communicative dimension of movement.

Delsarte believed the average adult incapable of producing a pure succession at will because of the inhibitions produced by restrictive social training at home and at school and by the prevalence of sport activities which set movement patterns. When Steele MacKaye began teaching Delsarte's principles in the United States, he developed Harmonic Gymnastics to free the body of obstacles to true successional movement. I am not advocating a revival of Harmonic Gymnastics, but I do believe that the concept of successions provides a perspective for understanding and, finally, freeing kinetic blocks.

If Delsarte's concept of true and reverse successions are accepted as guides, they can provide a useful beginning for certain aspects of a physical characterization. For example, a greedy character might be expected to have a dominant flow of movement from the outside toward his center. A general flow of gesture is suggested from this as well as some aspects of posture. More specifically, imagine the character of Fagan in *Oliver* as he instructs his boys on how to "pick a pocket or two." Think of Fagan's hands and fingers as he counts his gold pieces. The succession is predominantly from the outside toward the center.

The danger in considering this approach is, of course, in allowing the successional flow to replace motivation in playing actions, thereby producing the "stuck-on," stilted movement for which the Delsarte system was criticized at the beginning of the century. A concept must not replace characterization but rather serve that characterization where it can be motivated by the situation. Fagan's movements will not be confined to inward successions, but where such gesture is appropriate to the action of the scene an inward succession will communicate the intention of the gesture as well as enriching the texture of the characterization.

In summary, what has been attempted in this discussion is an integration of the widely varied movement experiences that comprise stage movement training. The concept of successional movement first defined by Delsarte and subsequently used by many others is just one perspective. It offers a point of view concerning the relationship of technical skill, physical facility, and physical characterization. The descriptions of successions in stage falls and rolls, sit-ups, the plow, standing round-overs, and in gesture and physical characterizations show how successional flow is related to specific movement situations.

From this basic introduction the next step is to discover successional flows in whatever approach to movement training you are now using. For the most part emphasizing successions which are a part of already existing movement sequences is sufficient. To meet an actor's specific need I have from time to time developed successional sequences, and you may want to do that as well. New relationships will become apparent as the potential of successional flow is explored, and it is these relationships that help integrate the varied physical disciplines which are encompassed by stage movement training.

PATRICIA RELPH *is an instructor at the University of Toledo and the Humanities Cluster College at Bowling Green State University. She directs, acts, and has taught acting for the past ten years. She is currently researching the physical and psychological bases of expressiveness and the developmental stages of the creative process.*

The Bodily Expression of Emotional Experience

by Patricia Relph

PERFORMING ARTISTS HAVE a special need to understand the body's fundamental expressiveness, from full body movement to subtle, visceral activity. Today when a performer prepares a role for stage or camera he is likely to rely exclusively on intuition or limited personal experience. Directors typically make decisions on characterization by the "this looks right and that doesn't" criterion. Today performing artists no longer need to depend exclusively on intuition. In this century great strides have been

29

made in the systematic study of the language of movement and its relation to personality, mood, etc. Psychologists have brought us quite close to an understanding of the mechanisms underlying the expression of psychological experience in muscular/glandular activity.

A clear and systematic understanding of the relationships between emotional experience and body use has been developed by two psychologists in this century: Wilhelm Reich (one of the great and, occasionally, notorious founders of modern psychology) and Alexander Lowen (a practicing psychiatrist, director of the Institute for Bioenergetic Analysis and author of seven important books). More than any others, they are responsible for the extensive and careful research which brings us new awareness of the somatic impact of mental experience.

Lowen and Reich are responsible for clarifying and naming five character types, which will be discussed here. Their understanding of the human character and how the psychological composition of a person is physically expressed is particularly important to the performer. Of course, narrow stereotyping of character is undesirable, but theatre artists must acknowledge that human behavior does fall into patterns and that those patterns do have significance. When a performer begins to work on a part he must decide how the inner character is to be expressed physically. He might begin by studying five basic character types. (A reaction to this might be, "But there are more than five kinds of people!") Of course humans develop in infinite variety; nevertheless, there is much evidence that individuals do exhibit patterns of behavior. There is also considerable evidence that the relationships between emotional experience and somatic behavior are very regular. Before an actor begins to study infinite variety, focus on simple patterns of expressive behavior might be profitable.

These five character types have evolved from thousands of hours of psychiatric clinical experience in which feeling and the resulting behavior patterns were studied. Within each pattern is all the latitude needed for the development of an individual character. The focus of Reich and Lowen's study is on those muscular/glandular behaviors which seem to be *regularly* linked to certain feelings and attitudes.

Systematic studies of this sort began with Sigmund Freud and his colleagues who perceived in their clinical work that emotional life and physical behaviors did not develop independently, but that the mode of body use seemed to be a response to the psychic experience. They found that physical behavior is in no way random, that it has clear structure, and that this structure correlates rather precisely with the individual's emotional structure. To say that these factors are "structured" is to say that the different behaviors are significantly related to each other, that an explanation of any factor requires an understanding of the other factors. A person is not a "collection" or "aggregate" of psychological and somatic behaviors, but rather a "system" of integrated behaviors, at least in the mind of the individual. Clearly, if such structures exist the actor could, indeed, profit by understanding them.

"Character" here means a fixed pattern of behavior; the typical way a person strives for what he wants in the world. Our character expresses itself in the way we look physically and the way we move through the world. Character is also a psychic structure composed of our hierarchy of shoulds, mustn'ts, want tos, aspirations, denials, taboos, rationalizations, and projections—all of which are geared to affirm our "ego ideal." Character is expressed in literally everything about us: our voice, our speech, all the choices we make in living.

Character structure can be ascertained from close study of the dynamics of the body structure (skin color, posture, muscular development, and tensions) and from patterns of voice and movement. The structure is seen not in the body that is given to us, but in how it is used by us.

Theatre artists are interested in all types of character, neurotic and healthy alike. (Figure 1 profiles a basically "normal" body stance.) Although many dramatic characters are healthy and normal, there are probably more who are neurotic or pathological. Therefore these character structures, which are heavily based on the study of moderately neurotic persons, are particularly useful to us. (This information can also help us understand the sources of the "bad acting" which is usually seen when a neurotic actor attempts to play a healthy character.)

FIGURE 1. *Normal*

After considerable observation of various character structures, Lowen systematically classified them into five character types. Each type was noted for a special pattern of defenses, on both the psychological and muscular level, that distinguished it from other types. This is a classification not of people but of defensive positions. No individual is a pure type, and every person in our culture combines in different degrees some or all of these defensive patterns. The performer's job is to learn how specific "defensive" positions are expressed somatically and in movement.

One need not be a therapist to recognize character types. Any average theatregoer unconsciously interprets character by noting how the performer moves and how he uses dialogue. After all, we do it constantly in everyday life. The trick for the theatre artist is to do this job consciously and precisely, and to know why this behavior suggests a particular character.

Five basic character types will be discussed—first, in terms of the psychological attitudes embodied in each of those types, and second, in terms of the accompanying physical traits. Finally the possible application of this information by the performer will be discussed.

A complete analysis of each character type is beyond our scope here; therefore each of the following types will be sketched only briefly. Even so, this information can provide the performer and director with insights into the fundamental body processes which express certain mental conditions. This information can serve as the foundation for the organic development of characterization.

The "Oral" Type

This character could also be called dependent, weak, or needy; he suffers from feelings of loss and deprivation. As an infant, in the oral stages of development, love and support were lacking, particularly contact with the mother's body. In adult life he experiences a feeling of inner emptiness and despair.

This character has greatly inhibited aggressiveness, feels the need to cling, and may show exaggerated signs of independence which break down under stress. The overall mood swings quickly from depression to elation. The body silhouette is usually long and thin with musculature underdeveloped, particularly in the arms and legs. The character's grounding (the ability to "stand on one's own feet," to "hold one's ground," to interact sensitively and spontaneously with one's environment) is diminished.

Weak grounding leads to insecure, unstable footing. The legs cease to sustain a sensitive and stable interaction with the ground. The spine becomes responsible for "holding the person up," and so it is inflexible and unavailable for the aggressive action needed to assert, to take, or to "stand one's ground." The spine is misaligned; there is usually a sway back (the top of the pelvis is rocked forward, the lower rib cage area is thrust forward; for weight compensation, the upper spine is pulled back and the shoulders are pulled forward and down).

The arms of the oral character are weak and underdeveloped because he does not make a physically strong effort to teach out for what he wants. If spontaneous reaching out for love is met with denial, he experiences pain. Soon he learns that each new denial enhances the sense of pain and aloneness and, thus, it seems safer not to reach out; however, the natural impulse to reach persists, and the effort to counteract the impulse adds to the pain and the sense of social alienation. The oral character concludes that the impulse itself must be suppressed. Since the impulse is spontaneous, it will continue unless feeling in the thoracic cavity, shoulders, and arms can be reduced.

Energetically the oral type is undercharged; enough energy is available to maintain vital functions, but not enough to charge the muscular system or reach the contact organs (head, hands, genitals, feet). Our energetic charge depends on full diaphragmatic breathing. In the oral type, and in all the other characters described herein, breathing is diminished. Shallow, partial breathing keeps this type in a weak, undercharged state, incapable of extended aggressive discharge. What causes diminished breathing? The more this type breathes, the more he feels. When he feels, the sense of longing and emptiness grows too painful to bear, so he must suppress the feeling. To suppress feeling one restricts his breathing, so the oral character retards the movement in the thorax and tightens the diaphragm: the collapse in the chest effectively prevents deep breathing. (See Figure 2, the oral stance.)

FIGURE 2. *Oral*

Characters in dramatic literature who seem to be oral types are: Estragon in *Waiting for Godot;* Claire in *A Delicate Balance;* the Actor and the Baron in Gorki's *The Lower Depths;* Mary in *A Long Day's Journey into Night;* and Laura in *The Glass Menagerie.* A certain helplessness and lack of aggression is an essential part of each of these characters. Caught in their own "child" states, each is incapable of taking mature, aggressive action on his or her own behalf. Each is in some way physically impaired in the feet and legs or is simply, as Gorki's Baron admits, "surrounded by a fog." Their helplessness, need, and inner despair are their most striking psychological features. (Of course each character suggests other dimensions which are not characteristic of the oral type. These particular characters are mentioned here because their most clearly expressed traits seem to indicate a basically oral nature.)

The "Masochistic" Type

This character type could also be called overburdened, for here the muscular system of the growing child is subverted from its natural function of spontaneous movement to that of holding. A large amount of the character's energy is invested in (1) holding back negative impulses (usually feelings of rage or hate directed against the parent figure) and (2) in holding back natural body functions (chiefly sexual and excremental). In this character, aggression and self-assertion are severely limited, but in a different way from the oral type. Grudging submissiveness is the dominant tendency while whining, complaining, and rationalizing are the main forms of self-assertion.

The physical characteristics of the masochistic type are a thick, bull neck and a rounded back. There is collapse in the waist, and the shoulders are pulled forward and down as if a burden were being carried across the shoulders and back. The shoulders are held tightly; the pelvis is tight and pushed forward. The buttocks are squeezed together, so the derriere is tight and flat. Although this body structure is not erect, the type tends to be somewhat strong muscularly—that is, heavy set and earthbound. The facial set is unique: usually it is an expression of naive innocence seen in (a very misleading) good natured smile. In this character, both aggressive and tender feelings are reduced. (See Figure 3.)

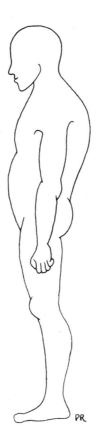

FIGURE 3. Masochistic

In *Waiting for Godot* Vladimir repeatedly exclaims "Nothing you can do about it" or "to every man his little cross, (sigh) 'till he dies. And is forgotten.'' In act two he wants to play the part of Lucky, the miserable slave introduced in act one. Vladimir's 'this is awful but nothing can be done about it' attitude strongly suggests a masochistic character structure. George in *Who's Afraid of Virginia Woolf* is another example of the same type. In the first moments of the script Albee repeatedly emphasizes George's passive resignation to Martha's authority. Albee notes in his stage directions that George is "defeated," "resigned and exasperated;" "George sulks," "George looks put upon." Later Martha says, ". . .you're such a simp! You don't even have the. . . ." George finishes her sentence with ". . .guts?" Tobias in *A Delicate Balance*, Willie in *Death of A Salesman*, and Clov in *Endgame* could also be considered masochistic types.

The ''Rigid'' Type

The rigid type combines three slightly different character structures: (1) the phallic/narcissistic (a male rigid type), (2) the compulsive (both male and female), and (3) the hysterical (a female rigid type). First the basic psychological and physical traits which normally indicate a rigid character will be described, and then the differences in the three will be covered.

This type is called rigid because it is based on a rigid ego or a strict set of taboos. The character is seen to possess a narrow mind combined with excessive pride, is afraid to give in, to appear weak, or to collapse, and thus remains continually on guard. He strictly holds back any impulse to open up or to reach out for tender human contact. This type is frequently seen to be highly ambitious, competitive, and vigorously aggressive.

The physical nature of the rigid type is unique because of the complete muscular armoring usually present. Armoring—a bio-energetic term describing habitual massive contraction of the large muscles near the surface of the body—is designed to: (1) restrain an impulse to expand or reach out, (2) hold the person together, or (3) make the person invulnerable (like the medieval knight's armor) to expected attacks from the outside. (Although all armoring is muscular tension, not all tension is armoring.)

This armoring in the rigid type, this massive chronic muscular tension, causes a loss of kinesthetic feedback, *i.e.* awareness of muscle behavior. The muscular surface of the rigid type is hard and inflexible to the touch. The rigid type has extremely limited awareness of the body and has succeeded in withholding most feeling except for the terrible pain of numbness itself.

In the general rigid stance the body is held stiff with pride: the head is high, the backbone straight and stiff. The body may look integrated and well-grounded, but lack of coordination and grace in movement is typical because the muscles of the hips, pelvis, shoulders, and face are tightly held. A solid jaw is aggressively set forward. (See Figure 4.)

The phallic / narcissistic character is a musclebound rigid type with much of his energy focusing on erective potency. This character is also quite stubborn. Dramatic characters such as Mack the Knife, Jean in *Miss Julie,* Henry VIII, Angelo in *Measure for Measure,* Oedipus, Nick in *Who's Afraid of Virginia Woolf,* and Stanley in *A Streetcar Named Desire* might be considered rigid types. These men are typically considered the strong, masculine type; it is that quality which the females in the script are attracted to. The sexual power of such men, especially in the conquest, is one of their major forms of self-expression. These are the men of power, sexual and otherwise; men for whom women and weaker men must assume a lesser position in the scheme of things.

The compulsive is a well known character, usually seen with a small, extremely tight muscular set, and is frequently associated with pedantry, avarice, and excessive desire for orderliness. Moliere's Miser is an excellent example of the compulsive type.

In females, the rigid type is most clearly seen in the hysterical

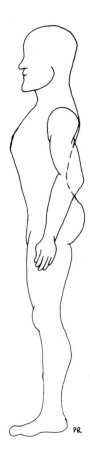

Figure 4. *Rigid (Phallic/Narcissistic)*

character. This character spends her energy enticing but is actually afraid to love, and her tender feelings are denied expression. In fact her total capacity for feeling is reduced. On the whole she remains guarded and tight; the psychic tightness corresponds to somatic tightness. Although the body has some agility for the purpose of sexual enticement, the main characteristic is one of overall physical armoring. The neck is stiff and unbending, as is the lower back. The head is held high

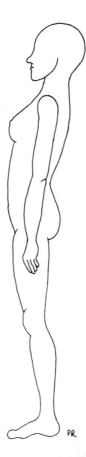

FIGURE 5. *Rigid (Hysterical)*

and the pelvis is sharply retracted. The front of the body is armored; the chest is stiffened (as if to meet an attack), but the arms are weak, incapable of much aggression. The breathing is sharply restricted because of a contracted diaphragm. A sense of pride and determination is seen in the strong, protruding jaw. This character is physically ungrounded, unstable on her feet because the legs are tight and rigid and the knees are locked. Usually she suffers from fear of falling. (See Figure 5.)

Strindberg's Miss Julie is a classic hysterical type. Her sexuality is shown as shockingly enticing, but beneath it is a deep fear and hatred of the male. ("I learnt from Mother to hate and distrust men. And I swore to her I'd never become the slave of any man.") Though not always by choice, Julie adheres to a rigid set of laws for living. In her "dream" speech she discloses: ". . . I'm on top of a pillar and can't see any way of getting down." Later she declares: "I haven't anything that's my own. I haven't one single thought that I didn't get from my father, one emotion that didn't come from my mother. . . ." Julie's rigid pride prevents her from feeling guiltless. Her hysterical shame and helplessness facilitate her taking the dreaded role of "slave." She cries: "Oh my God, what have I done?" Jean replies, "Same as many before you." Julie answers (hysterically): "And now you despise me. I'm falling, I'm falling." Although Julie is seen to possess tremendous psychic energy, she is incapable of taking aggressive action on her own behalf. At the end of the play she cries, "I can't do anything. Can't be sorry, can't run away, can't stay, can't live—can't die. Help me. Order me and I'll obey like a dog." Many other female characters in dramatic literature could be seen as hysterical types, including Blanche DuBois in *A Streetcar Named Desire*, Julia in *A Delicate Balance*, and Beatrice in *The Effect of Gamma Rays On Man-in-the-Moon Marigolds*.

The "Psychopathic" Type

This person's basic attitude is a denial of human feeling; he characteristically rejects his own body and feelings, especially sexual feelings. He is driven to acquire power, feels the need to dominate others, and will either bully or seduce to achieve objectives. This character cannot admit defeat.

The physical types of the psychopathic character fall into two categories, the overpowering and the seductive. The overpowering version is physically large with a big energy investment in the upper part of the body, especially the head, and very little energy investment in the lower half of the body. The diaphragm is tightly constricted, and the pelvis and head are held tightly, which makes the top half of the body appear heavy and rigid while the lower half appears narrow and weak. The face is usually distrustful, with watchful eyes. (See Figure 6.)

FIGURE 6. *Psychopathic*

The seductive type usually appears to have a normal body, although he may have a hyperflexible back, combined with a loose and overcharged pelvis. Great tension in the head and eyes is frequently observed.

Dramatic characters such as Shakespeare's Richard III and Iago are vivid examples of the psychopathic type. In *Henry VI, Part 3* (Act III, Scene 3) the young Richard reveals himself in a moving soliloquy.

"Why then, I do but dream on sovereignty;
Like one that stands upon a promontory,
And spies a far-off shore where he would tread,
Wishing his foot were equal with his eye;
And chides the sea that sunders him from thence,
Saying, he'll lade it dry to have his way:
So do I wish the crown. . .

". . . love forswore me in my mother's womb:
And, for I should not deal in her soft laws,
She did corrupt frail nature with some bribe,
To shrink mine arm up like a wither'd shrub;
To make an envious mountain on my back,
Where sits deformity to mock my body;
To shape my legs of an unequal size; . . .
And am I then a man to be belov'd?
O monstrous fault! to harbour such a thought.
Then, since this earth affords no joy to me. . .
I'll make my heaven to dream upon the crown;
And whiles I live, to account this world but hell. . ."

In *Othello* (Act I, Scene 1) Iago bluntly discloses:

". . .Others there are
Who, trimm'd in forms and visages of duty,
Keep yet their hearts attending on themselves,
And, throwing but shows of service on their lords,
Do well thrive by them, and when they have lin'd their coats
Do themselves homage: These fellows have some soul;
And such a one do I profess myself."

Richard and Iago use both the overpowering and the seductive approach to achieve their ends. The same is true of Martha in *Who's Afraid of Virginia Woolf,* who—in the first scene—orders her guests with, "I said c'mon in! Now c'mon!" Later she seduces Nick, "Now, for being such a good boy, you can give me a kiss. C'mon. . . a friendly kiss. C'mon." In act three Martha speaks her famous line, "You're all flops. I am the Mother Earth and you're all flops." Other dramatic characters who may be considered psychopathic types and who use either the overpowering or seductive approach (and sometimes both) are: King Claudius in *Hamlet;* Ferdinand in *The Duchess of Malfi;* Hedda in *Hedda Gabler;* Vassilisa in *The Lower Depths;* and the Peachums in Brecht's *The Threepenny Opera.*

The "Schizoid" Type

This type should not be confused with a schizophrenic. The common schizoid character suffers from a much milder form of dissociation between ego and body than does the schizophrenic. His thinking is dissociated from feeling and behavior, and contact with the body and feeling is greatly reduced. The energy charge never reaches the contact organs, but remains frozen in the center unless a big energy build-up causes a violent explosion. Even the circulation of the blood is diminished, causing the skin to be pale and cold. There is frequently a split in attitudes: arrogance/debasement or virginal/sluttish. There is always a strong avoidance of intimate feelings.

The physical traits of the schizoid types are these: the body is narrow, contracted, rigid, and brittle. The main tensions are at the base of the skull, the shoulder joints, the pelvis joint, the leg joints, and the diaphragm. Usually the diaphragm tension is severe, causing a split in the body to occur. The top half and the lower half of the body seem to belong to two different people. The breathing is very shallow and weak. The face is mask-like, while the arms hang like dead appendages. The feet are contracted and the grounding poor. (See Figure 7.)

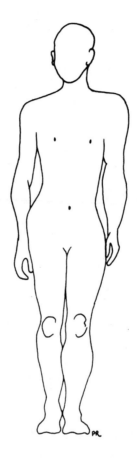

FIGURE 7. *Schizoid*

The schizoid structure takes a variety of physical shapes. This character type results from a lifetime of conflict and struggle. Many highly neurotic characters, especially those who have "cut themselves off" from their bodies and feelings, like Brecht's Arturo Ui, Hamm in *Endgame*, and Charlotte Corday in *Marat/Sade*, are predominantly schizoid types.

Application of Structures to Actor Training

These character structure categories represent useful ways of describing the relationship between: (1) causes, (2) psychological experience, and (3) behavior. The character structures described here represent frequently observed modes of human behavior and experience. Of course this is not the only way of looking at human experience, nor are these types meant to explain the vast possibilities of unique human behavior. It is rare that a person will embody only the characteristics of one type.

Theatre artists can use this information in the reverse of the way in which the psychologist uses it. The latter studies the body behavior in order to understand the workings of the mind. The job of the performer and the director is to interpret the character's inner experience, find its determinants, and then discover the somatic impact of the experience. On stage, the performer's task is to recreate that somatic impact within the body.

These character descriptions are concerned with basic body attitudes; they are a starting point for theatre artists. The performer wants to create a character whose physical appearance and behavior is specific, economic, and suggestive of a full and complex inner life, and Lowen and Reich's systematic outline of basic human characteristics is a rich resource for theatre artists attempting to bring characters to life with honesty and clarity. The character studies are useful for persona in both realistic and stylized plays. Stylized drama is abstracted from real behavior, and it is precisely the fundamental physical and psychic behaviors discussed here which become the foundation of the stylized characters after naturalistic irrelevancies have been stripped away.

There are two ways in which this information may be helpful to the performer, first as a method for finding an appropriate physical characterization, and second as a method of tapping inner feeling. In order to develop a physical characterization, attention is placed on vital areas of the body such as the feet, pelvis, shoulders, and chest, so that the performer starts to build the character from the center and radiate outward. How many characters can be seen on today's stage whose main expressors are only the arms, or who use behavior entirely inappropriate for the character implied in the script?

There is a difference between a performer's use of this kind of information and the more superficial imitation which fails to yield a convincing characterization. The performer should not try to look like the character, but should rather feel the character's fears and then make use of the character's defenses. He doesn't try to act stiff, but tightens the front of the body to meet the expected attack.

When a performer must experience a peak moment in the drama, and must communicate big feelings such as rage, fear, disgust, or sorrow, a rich repertoire of behaviors and a systematic way of choosing appropriate behavior is now available. For example, a person experiencing sudden fear might respond with any or all of these behaviors: a sharp intake of breath (coupled with massive armoring of the thorax which prohibits free breathing), eyes widen, head pulls in, shoulders rise, buttocks tighten, legs lock, and the whole body retracts and tightens. The intensity of these behaviors depends on the nature of the character. This example of fear responses represents a thorough and systematic base upon which one may begin physicalization work.

Secondly, knowledge of physical types can also aid the actor by providing an outline through which inner feelings may be tapped; the actor moves from the expression to the feeling. When a person, for example, experiences a sudden intake of breath, an armored thorax, and bulging eyes, these somatic experiences will almost certainly evoke the emotional response of fear because of the muscle memories held within our bodies.

A performer can adopt the behavior of the character type and still work with full organic authenticity; using the character structure approach should not lead to external manipulation. Because the somatic and psychic activity are closely correlated, the performer who suppresses the breathing will begin to feel the fear.

It is hoped that by means of an introduction to this area of human behavior, theatre artists might be alerted to the research of psychologists—particularly Reich and Lowen. Currently in the theatre there is great interest and considerable research in body awareness, movement, and total body development techniques. We will surely profit by our study of all aspects of human behavior, since it is our job to create honest, moving images of human experience.

BIBLIOGRAPHY

Alexander, F.M. *The Resurrection of the Body.* New York: Dell Publishing Co., 1974.

Baker, E. *Man in the Trap.* New York: Macmillan Co., 1967.

Energy and Character, a British journal, edited by David Boadella.

Feldenkrais, M. *Awareness Through Movement.* New York: Harper and Row, 1972.

_____. *Body and Mature Behavior.* New York: International Universities Press, 1970.

Kurtz, R., and Prestera, H. *The Body Reveals.* New York: Harper and Row, 1976.

Lowen, A. *The Betrayal of the Body,* New York: Macmillan Co., 1967.

_____. *Bioenergetics.* New York: Penguin Books, 1975.

_____. *The Language of the Body.* New York: Macmillan Co., 1971. (Originally published as *The Physical Dynamics of Character Structure.* New York: Grune and Stratton, 1958.)

Reich, W. *Character Analysis.* New York: Farrar, Straus and Giroux, Noonday Press, 1972. (Originally published in New York by Orgone Institute Press, 1949.)

Rolf, I. *Structural Integration.* New York: Viking/Esalen, 1975.

LINDA CONAWAY *is an assistant professor at Miami University in Oxford, Ohio. At Miami she teaches movement and costume design and is the resident costume designer and choreographer. She is a member of United Scenic Artists of America and Author's League of America. In addition to undergraduate work at Stephens College and graduate work at the University of Missouri her training includes eighteen years of dance and gymnastics, seven years of study in Si Lum Pai, and T'ai Chi.*

Image, Idea, and Expression: T'ai Chi and Actor Training

by Linda Conaway

MOVEMENT TRAINING is a major concern for today's actor. Much of his training is a combination of dance, gymnastics, and fencing for the body which tends to separate the body from the mind. One discipline actors are using to help integrate the mind and body is that of T'ai Chi. The following discussion is not a "how to" guide, but rather an introduction to the philosophy, movement principles, and some basic movements of T'ai Chi as an effective addition to the actor's movement training program.

51

The origin of T'ai Chi is obscured by Chinese myth and folk-lore. Some believe it to be the creation of the Taoists who lived close to the earth and let things take their natural course, unlike modern man who is inclined to interfere. Others believe this art to be a creation of ancient Chinese soldiers as a means of balancing and expanding their severe physical training to include the development of the mind, patience, awareness, and sensitivity to the opponent's rhythms and tensions. Today in monasteries throughout China, monks practice T'ai Chi which over the course of history has been passed down from one generation to another. This accounts for the wide number of forms (combinations of prescribed movement motif) practiced today. The literature of this art is the *I Ching, Book of Changes* and the *Tao Te Ching*—a series of poems which explore the paradoxes of life and nature. Frequently Ta'ai Chi is erroneously grouped with the self-defense arts because both acts involve a sense of flow, movement, and awareness of self. The practice of T'ai Chi as a means of self-defense is called T'ai Chi Ch'uan, while T'ai Chi is more appropriately grouped with the various methods of meditation.

What is T'ai Chi? It is a form of meditation, a healing process, and an art form. As meditation, T'ai Chi clears the mind of clutter, imposed goals, and tension, and allows for incoming knowledge. T'ai Chi brings harmony to the mind and body. As a healing process, T'ai Chi accomplishes the continuous flow of breath with both movement and mind working together in harmony. Through practice, blocks to the natural flow and rhythm of the physical self become apparent, and for this reason T'ai Chi is sometimes used as a healing process for arthritis and for various ailments of the joints, muscles, and breath. T'ai Chi is also an art form which can be experienced by the observer and practitioner. For the observer it is an art by virtue of the shapes visualized in space created by the movements of the body. The pleasure derived by the onlooker is similar to the pleasure experienced watching a folk dance or any other carefully choreographed dance. For the practitioner, T'ai

Chi becomes an individual art form because no two people perform it in the same fashion. New discoveries are made in each practice which encourage the creative process.

Essence in T'ai Chi is finding and fixing that point at which thought becomes action and action, thought (yin-yang). Complementary opposites merge in total balance, simultaneity, and unity. The yin-yang sign symbolizes the underlying principles of T'ai Chi as a moving art to develop awareness. (See Figure 1.)

FIGURE 1. *Yin-Yang*

Note the apparent balance and contrast in Figure 1 with the presence of all color on the left and the total absence of color in the other half. In T'ai Chi, as in the yin-yang symbol, we find a balance between thinking and doing. Western man is encouraged to analyze all things while T'ai Chi teaches us to do, to experience, to understand, and accept without analysis. In dance training and other physical training with obvious rhythm, the student is taught to count and fit the movement to the music as in a prescribed mold. Restrictions on physical activity and molding begins early in primary school where children are asked to sit quietly for extended periods of time. Boys are taught to be expressive in outward ways which lack physical subtlety while girls are taught to cross their legs and be demure. From the day of birth we are squeezed and glued, snipped and taped, pared and shrunken to fit the mold. Years later, the young actor must unlearn the restrictions and rediscover free expression. T'ai Chi holds the promise of an effective way of confronting and alleviating common restrictive problems because it allows us to be free and rediscover the natural flow and joy of movement.

T'ai Chi accomplishes a kind of unique unity. As a symbol for T'ai Chi the yin-yang sign itself is a unified picture even though it is made of contrasting color and shape. Like many things in nature made of contrasting parts, the sign when viewed as a whole has a kind of unity. T'ai Chi, like the yin-yang sign, encourages unity and wholeness of the person. It is much like a wheat field in the wind with each shaft of wheat moving independently and in its own space and rhythm, yet the field as a whole presents a unified picture.

In addition to balance and centering T'ai Chi teaches us to accept constant change. The yin is change and the yang is constant, which in itself explains one of life's greatest polarities in the statement ''the only constant is change.'' The acceptance and recognition of this constant change is one of the bases for the T'ai Chi method of discovering spontaneity. Through daily practice of T'ai Chi, one finds changing sources of energy (centers) as well as changing body rhythms and energy boundaries. One learns to maintain a freshness of discovery through energy regeneration and re-creation.

T'ai Chi accomplishes many goals for both the actor and the teacher. While dance, gymnastics, fencing, and karate exercise the muscles, tissues, and exterior of the physical body, T'ai Chi exercises the inner organs as well. T'ai Chi also helps the student accomplish total unity of his physical being, his breathing, rhythm, and movement.

Energy and Posture

Finding one's energy and correct posture are natural benefits of regular practice of T'ai Chi. Unlike many forms of dance which ask the body to pull up and away from the ground, this art form requires a stable, strong connection with the earth.

- The student should begin at the head and work down the neck, over the shoulders, out the arms to the fingertips, and continue down the spine releasing any muscle not needed to maintain a standing posture.

Think only of releasing and giving in to gravity. In this manner tension flows away from the body and into the earth. Always allow the head to rest lightly on the top vertebrae. Full release has been accomplished when the body springs back into place if pushed down from the head. Thinking of the body as a piece of foam which returns to its original shape when squeezed and released is a helpful image.

As in meditation, the breath should circulate. All breath and movement begins in the "tant ien"—that point in the lower abdomen right below the navel—and circulates throughout the entire body. This point is the reservoir of energy and center from which all movement stems. Finally, the student inhales and thinks of extending the spine upward and widens it from left to right. He should follow the breath flow and its natural coordination with the movement.

T'ai Chi encourages the actor to discover the physiological center of his person because all activity grows out of the center (tant ien). In applying the teaching and movements of T'ai Chi the actor not only intellectually understands the center but utilizes it in motion. T'ai Chi proposes a theory in direct opposition to that of articulating a body image and then imposing this image on oneself. The actor must work with many extraneous factors: script rhythm, director's rhythm, the individual "character's" rhythm, as well as guided placement. How can he accurately and successfully deal with these opposing factors without the complete understanding of her or his own personal rhythm? The successful use of T'ai Chi is one method of discovering this individual rhythm.

Meditation

As a form of meditation the following process or manner of clearing the mind is fundamental to the practice of T'ai Chi.

- Begin by allowing thoughts to pass through one's mind like wind in a field. Find a comfortable sitting position with the spine straight (never rigid), and place the head lightly on your spine.
- Next, begin to "circulate the Chi." The Chi is the light, so try to imagine the breath as a shaft of light. Inhale and allow the light to enter and then circulate from the abdomen to the head, arms, fingertips, spine, and legs. Exhale and let the light escape, only to return with the next inhalation. Raise the spine with the inhalation and descend with exhalation, but do not let the back collapse.

Concentrate on this circulation of the Chi. Once this becomes a felt experience, allow the environment (sounds, scents, etc.) to pass through awareness and let the breathing take over. This preliminary practice results in relaxation, slowing down of body activity, and general release of tension (Wu Wei). The T'ai Chi approach to meditation is not dependent on solitude, for it can be done anywhere, at any time, and in any comfortable posture which allows for a straight spine. Two favorite standing positions for meditation are the universal post (Figure 2) and the horse stance (Figure 3).

THE UNIVERSAL POST

The universal post is an upright position with the weight on the right foot; the other foot is extended in front, lightly touching the ground. The knees should be relaxed and the arms extended in front with relaxed elbows as if grasping a fence post.

FIGURE 2. *Universal Post*

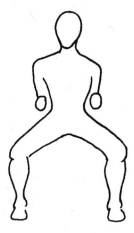

FIGURE 3. *Horse Stance*

THE HORSE STANCE

The horse stance is another upright stance. The feet are set in a wide, parallel second position with knees bent comfortably directly over the toes, the back is straight, and the hands are in loose fists extending straight from the forearm resting at the hip bone. When the T'ai Chi meditation begins to work within the student, he is ready to move into a slow, easy study of a particular form. Daily practice develops patience, concentration, and awareness.

Tui Sho

Two particular problems of the actor are balance and centering. In T'ai Chi achieving unity and harmony of self in movement equals centering. Balance and centering are not intellectual achievements but rather a natural benefit resulting from correct practice of T'ai Chi. The focal center of any movement is the total body. When one is most centered there occurs a sense of both sides of the circle (Chi) simultaneously. Furthermore, one should maintain an awkward central spine so one is able to return to a home base. The concept of the awkward spine is best understood through a tree trunk image.

- Imagine a tree trunk extending from the center point between the feet up to the crown of your head. Never consider movement left or right, but rather consider all movement as an outgrowth of this trunk.

To test the balance and center find a partner. Stand facing each other, adapt a comfortable stance, place palms together, and push. Without establishing a rhythmic or behavior pattern, randomly release the hands from those of the partner and vice versa. If either partner senses a faltering in breath or balance, then the centering is not total. This exercise with two people working together in a supportive way is called pushing hands, and it is the first exercise in the study of Tui Sho which, in T'ai Chi, teaches trust—an important lesson for all actors. Pushing hands is demonstrated in Figure 4.

There are many variations of Tui Sho. Two of the most effective are a pulse connecting motif and a circling hands motif.

- In the pulse connecting motif, two partners stand facing each other and touch wrists, pulse points together. To begin, one person must initiate the movement of making circles in the air with his hands, the other must follow, and soon the action will merge—without either partner serving as leader or follower. One will become attuned to the rhythm of the other, and the partners will trust each other. This particular variation, the pulse connecting motif, is known as pushing wrists and is demonstrated in Figure 5.

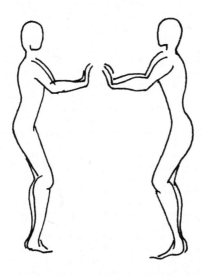

FIGURE 4. *Tui Sho (Pushing Hands)*

- A second variation, the circling hands motif, is performed in the same manner as pushing wrists—except that now the palms instead of the wrists are touching. When making circles, explore surrounding space and levels. As trust between partners develops, movement will become more free. Try to approach the exercise with joy, rather than with solemnity.

Frequently teachers of T'ai Chi practice Tui Sho while speaking or singing at the same time as their partner, and the two eventually become as one—speaking or singing the same sounds, rhythms, and tones.

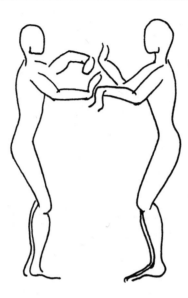

FIGURE 5. *Tui Sho (Pushing Wrists)*

Tui Sho teaches trust, and it develops a sensitivity to the forces of our opponents. In both forms of these martial arts, and in many traditional actor training approaches, the student is asked to meet force with force. In T'ai Chi one transforms force into energy and learns to become yielding and non-resistant. Instead of resisting force, the student accepts it, translates it into energy, and lets it go. The participant discovers where and how he is resistant and learns how the natural energy flow is disrupted. He becomes the reflection of his partner and makes discoveries about his own attitudes and body characteristics through the partner's reflection.

Storage and Energy

Storage is the basis for the T'ai Chi method of using energy. Energy is released through every pore, and like a boomerang it circles and returns, then is stored and reused. It is somewhat akin to a child's paddleball going away and then returning. This use of energy prevents fatigue and anxiety because it is recycled. The following exercise will encourage energy release:

- Stand with arms extended in front, allow the energy to escape from the fingertips, then make a large circle with the arms and sense the circle of energy surrounding oneself. (See Figure 6.)

FIGURE 6. *Broken line indicates direction of movement and circle of energy*

From the exterior the body may appear still. The energy flow, however, is in constant circulation—the internal is never still. To think of stillness creates tension and rigidity. Energy is constant action and yet retains quietness within and an apparent stillness. T'ai Chi energy is action, and it occurs when we allow it to happen rather than when we consciously work toward a specific goal. After all the previous exercises have become a real experience for the student, he is ready to begin a slow, easy study of a form and work toward continuous flow. The slow pace develops an awareness of the subtleties of movement and the environment. Always exhale before beginning. Any form is something to be worked *with*. The doer controls the form rather than being controlled by the form. He does his own T'ai Chi.

Opening Move

- The first T'ai Chi movement is very simple: Standing in the correct posture, allow the arms to rise (feeling the resistance of the air) and fall (feeling the same resistance). Allow the body to sink into the earth while inhaling and raising the arms; the arms descend while exhaling. (See Figure 7.)

FIGURE 7. *Opening Move (broken line indicates direction of movement)*

Do not allow a specified movement to limit movement and remember that each movement is only one expression of a whole. Play with the opening move in space and direction until it becomes an organic, comfortable experience. Always keep the weight between the feet and maintain a constant, firm connection with the earth. Up to this point all movement has been without changing base.

T'ai Chi Walk

Next, make the T'ai Chi walk a part of yourself. For this walk use the entire foot and allow the steps to be soft and resilient.

- The feet and legs should have a strong, stable connection with the earth. The spine is straight, knees bent and

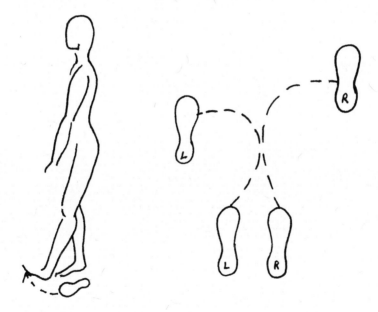

FIGURE 8. *T'ai Chi Walk (body positions before weight shift)*

FIGURE 9. *Circular step pattern of T'ai Chi walk*

relaxed, with feet parallel. The feet move in alternating circular steps; the head remains level. (See Figures 8 and 9.)

Play with the walk, travel in all directions, and eventually return to your original place. Next, allow the breath to follow the flow. This is the first experience in T'ai Chi as a moving meditation. Allow the scents, sounds, and sights to pass through your awareness (like images passing in front of a mirror).

Wild Horse Tossing Mane

The third motif, known as wild horse tossing mane, is based on the image of a large beach ball.

FIGURE 10. *Wild Horse Tossing Mane (arrows indicate directions of movement)*

- Begin by facing front in a horse stance. Turn the left heel out and twist the torso to the right. As you twist your torso imagine yourself holding a deflated beach ball which grows as you carry it. The right hand is on the top of the ball and the left hand is on the bottom. Carry this beach ball around in front of you. During this phase of the motif you inhale slowly.
- Shift your weight to the right foot and take a T'ai Chi step with the left. As you shift your weight, squeeze the air out and stretch the ball like taffy to your left diagonal. The T'ai Chi step marks the beginning of the exhale.
- Shift your weight back to the right foot and repeat this pattern to the left. This motif (one specified movement from a form) should be repeated three times. (See Figure 11.)

Figure 11. *Wild Horse Tossing Mane (body position when stretching the ball)*

Cloud Hands

The fourth motif, cloud hands, is another excellent motif for the actor who does not have a coach to guide him through an entire form but who wishes to experiment and to experience T'ai Chi.

- Begin in a horse stance, facing front; take one step to the left side each time the left hand circles. Slide your right foot to meet the left each time the right hand circles. Make a large circle with the right hand and then with the left.

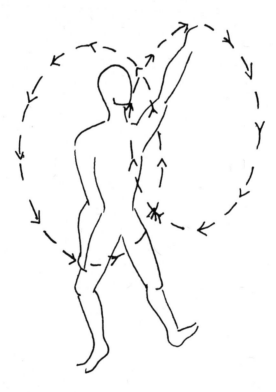

FIGURE 12. *Cloud Hands Body Position (broken lines indicate movement pattern)*

Visual focus should be on the working hand. Inhale with the left circle and exhale with the right. This is commonly repeated three times. (See Figures 12 and 13.)

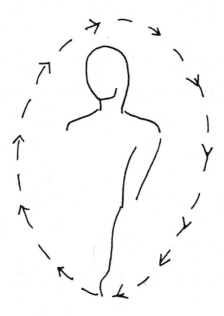

FIGURE 13. *Cloud Hands (the first circle)*

Like all movement training, everything should be practiced to both the left and right sides. These motifs should be approached with a childlike innocence and an open mind. Each time a prescribed movement is initiated, try to approach it in the present time, not as it was executed yesterday or five minutes ago. Experience each movement anew with each practice. In working cloud hands, sense the space between the body and arms, because the use and awareness of space depends on sensitivity to the surrounding air and its resistance. Practice in water increases sensitivity to resistance and will develop flow and a floating quality desirable in the practice of T'ai Chi. The eyes always follow the forward hand. All T'ai Chi movements are variations of these circular themes. Work these four motifs (opening move, T'ai Chi walk, wild horse tossing mane, and cloud hands) in any combination, varying the range and scope of the movement each time. When a transition is needed, invent one. With each practice session the motifs should grow rather than merely imitate what was previously achieved. Let one movement flow into the next without hesitation or sudden change. Avoid thoughts such as, "what comes next?" or "how many times is this repeated?" If such thoughts come to mind, take time to erase them and begin again.

There is no one way to approach a form. Each practitioner develops his own form, which is based on a framework of movement patterns. However, an understanding of the principles and the philosophy is primary to the successful acquisition of the T'ai Chi art. One should try to avoid concentration on specific details of movement because these will vary from individual to individual anyway. And never practice by counting. One must learn, as one must teach, from one's own experience in the here and now and not from one's memory of how one once learned or was once taught. For each day our experience, our images, change and grow.

As a training method, T'ai Chi should be approached with innocence and wonder—one *allows* it to happen. If a goal is imposed, or if movements are analyzed and qualified, the experience is voided. But if a student approaches it in the manner suggested, *allowing* the experience to happen, he will find that the experience will become part of himself. And if a teacher approaches T'ai Chi training by taking the time to prepare the student, he will find that the entire T'ai Chi approach can be applied to many different experiences—for a student trained in T'ai Chi will spend a great deal of time exploring and experimenting without fear of ugly movements or improper timing. An actor, for example, may begin to use a more open and innocent approach to character study; he will begin to control the script rather than allowing the script to control him.

Beginning enthusiasts frequently ask what music should be used to create a mood or to block out distraction. The best accompaniment is the available sounds of the environment or, perhaps even better, the sound of nature, taped at random. Chanting is another possibility. Let the jaw relax and drop, allowing the sound to flow. Chanting is especially nice if one is working in a space with other people. But whatever is used in the way of music, one should—as a good jazz musician does— allow the music to become part of the experience. Do not dance or move *to* the music; dance or move *within* it.

In the movement training program, the form of T'ai Chi is not of primary importance. As a training tool, T'ai Chi should not be approached as a memorization of certain motions, because this in itself means little. It is irrelevant whether one creates his own form, uses an already established form, or reflects fragments of complete forms. What matters is that training should begin with the individual and, eventually, be expanded to the external forms of body training. An actor's movement training is not complete without both the external and the internal. The extension of essence plus form (karate, dance, mime, fencing, and gymnastics) plus skills (dramatic action, phrasing or pace, projection, and visibility) yields versatility and total body awareness, effective body image, and execution of the intellect.

SEARS A. ELDREDGE *is associate professor of drama and chairman of the drama department at Earlham College in Richmond, Indiana. In his dissertation he has researched the teaching of masks in several important actor training programs in the United States.*

HOLLIS W. HUSTON *is an assistant professor at the University of Delaware where he teaches mask and mime for actors. He has studied and researched movement training methods and written articles on mime and actor training for the* Educational Theatre Journal *and other publications.*

Actor Training in the Neutral Mask

by Sears A. Eldredge
and Hollis W. Huston

IN PARIS, during the first World War, Jacques Copeau developed the idea of a severe and simple form of theatre, neither classical nor topical, but versatile through the economy of its means. In 1919 he remodeled the stage of the Vieux-Columbier in accordance with his new ideas, and over the next two years he founded a school for the training of actors, the Ecole du Vieux Columbier. Both in design and in acting, Copeau wanted to make large statements with simple gestures. The pursuit

71

of simplicity made him eliminate distractions, to create the still ground against which a movement or a form could be seen. His bare architectural stage was meant to magnify the evanescent statements of the drama. "I want the stage to be naked and neutral," he wrote, "in order that every delicacy may appear there, in order that every fault may stand out; in order that the dramatic work may have a chance in this neutral atmosphere to fashion that individual garment which it knows how to put on."[1] The simplicity that Copeau sought required a neutral atmosphere.

Copeau built that atmosphere into the theatrical space of the Vieux-Columbier, but to realize it in the spaces and rhythms of the actor's body was another, less tangible problem. The actor would have to be stripped as bare as the stage; only then could he express himself clearly and simply. Otherwise, the movement would be lost against a ground of temperament or convention. To find the neutral atmosphere within himself, therefore, the actor would first have to give up deeply ingrained but superficial habits. "The actor always starts from an artificial attitude, a bodily, mental, or vocal grimace. His attack is both too deliberated and insufficiently premeditated."[2] The starting point was to be not an attitude but a silence serving as a resting state, a condition without motion but filled with energy, like the condition of a runner in the moment before his race. All impulses were to arise from that state and return to it. "To start from silence and calm. That is the very first point. An actor must know how to be silent, to listen, to answer, to remain motionless, to start a gesture, follow through with it, come back to motionlessness and silence, with all the shadings and half-tones that these actions imply."[3]

To lead actors into familiarity with a neutral atmosphere in their own bodies, Copeau assigned his students to work with masks. In Copeau's use of the mask to rid the actor of temperamental habits, Etienne Decroux found the germ of his severe and abstractive corporeal mime. Decroux noticed that the mask reveals the personality of the wearer. In commonplace actions as well as dramatic ones, the actor's idiosyncratic way of moving tended to drown the movement itself: under the mask *how* becomes more important than *what.* "So we're relying on masks to fix things up, are we? But it's just the contrary! Masks make things worse. . . . It's like lightning. We see everything you do clearly. And the moment you wear a mask, especially [a neutral] mask, we see the quality of what you're doing."[4] If the mask could reveal the "attitude" or "grimace" that controlled the untrained actor, then it could also amplify and objectify the "neutral atmosphere" when the actor found it. Therefore, the neutral mask became an important tool for Copeau and for a later generation of teachers.

Copeau's school did not survive, but the influence of his mask training has been carried on in two main channels. One of those channels was defined by Michel Saint-Denis, Copeau's nephew; the other, by Jacques Lecoq, who trained under Jean Daste, Copeau's son-in-law, from 1945 to 1947. Teachers from both traditions have worked in or founded actor training programs in the United States. The Saint-Denis teaching stresses the actor's service to text and uses only character masks, though some of those are closer to neutrality than others. Lecoq's teaching, on the other hand, is concerned in its initial phase with matters that precede speech and character. Before wearing character masks, Lecoq's students are made familiar with the *masque neutre,* which is designed to rid them of conditioned attitudes in favor of an economical use of the body. More than any other person, Lecoq has defined the neutral state for the performer, as it is realized in masks.

Neutrality

Jacques Lecoq speaks of the neutral mask as tending toward a "fulcrum point which doesn't exist." As the actor approaches this fixed point, he becomes "a blank sheet of paper, a 'tabula rasa.' "[5] For Bari Rolfe, "the two words, 'appropriate' and 'economical' together almost add up to the term 'neutral.' "[6]

"The student executes any action, like walking, with only the expenditure of energy and rhythm, in space and in time, that the action requires."[7] Richard Hayes-Marshall speaks of neutrality as "a condition such that, if the actor finds himself there, he doesn't know what he will do next. . . . When you are there, you don't know what it is; if you did, it wouldn't be neutral."[8] Andrew Hepburn writes that "Neutrality means responding to stimuli in a *purely sensory* way."[9]

A neutral organism expends only the energy required by the task at hand. Personalities expend that amount of energy and something else besides; personalities are distinguished from each other by nature of what they add. Therefore, to be a personality, to be oneself even, is not to be neutral. Yet one cannot avoid being oneself. An actor can hope to perform a neutral action, but he cannot be neutral— neutral is a "fulcrum point that doesn't exist." To approach neutral action, one must lose oneself, denying one's own attitudes or intentions. At the moment of neutral action, one does not know what one will do next, because anticipation is a mark of personality; one cannot describe how one feels because introspection intrudes on simplicity; one reacts in a sensory way, because when the mind stops defining experience, the senses still function. Economy demands that both motion and rest be unpremeditated. Neutral activity withholds nothing; it is an energized condition, like the moment of inspiration before speech. The neutrality that the mask seeks is an economy of mind and body, evidenced at rest, in motion, and in the relationship between them.

Characteristics of the Masks

The personality of the maskmaker threatens the neutrality of the mask. One must devote many trials and experiments to the research of neutrality. Hayes-Marshall has redesigned his neutral masks seven times. "There is no such thing as a neutral mask," he says, "It has to be designed by somebody."

Neutral masks are at rest; they do not gesture, frown, smile, or grimace. The masks are symmetrical. Though the neutral mask is never used for speaking, the lips are lightly parted, as if the mask were about to speak. The masks are usually designed in pairs, male and female. Since the male and female bodies have different centers of gravity, the masks that will be carried by them must also differ. The leather mask designed for Lecoq by Sartori is brown, but celastic or papier-mache masks used in other studios are often white. A white mask reflects light well, and therefore shows its expression clearly; brown masks, on the

FIGURE 1. *Male and female neutral masks designed by Richard Hayes-Marshall, strongly influenced by the Sartori originals*

other hand, are closer in appearance to skin tones. Leather is the best material for simulating the textures of living skin, but there are few people capable of making leather masks. Amleto Sartori of Padua reconstructed the craft from Renaissance sources and made neutral, expressive, and *commedia* masks of leather for Lecoq and for Carlo Mazzone-Clementi. His son Donato carries on the work today, but the masks are expensive and take time to produce. Papier-maché or celastic masks are easier and cheaper.

Styles of sculpting vary according to the amount of personality considered proper in the mask. The Sartori mask used by Lecoq, which is dominated by a pair of sharp lines that define the nose and continue upward to form the brow line, seems to some observers rather abstract (Figure 1). The Hepburn mask (Figure 2) is softer in outline and more naturalistic: detailed contours in the nose, eyes, cheeks, and brows give an impression of flesh and muscle. The tragic masks of the Saint-Denis tradition, which are used for some of the same purposes as the neutral mask, are simple and harmonious masks that represent the four ages of man.[10] At the extreme of abstraction is the metaphysical mask of Mazzone-Clementi (Figure 3). The metaphysical mask is defined only by a center line, brow line, and one circular and one triangular eye hole. An abstract mask leads the actor beyond psychology to the intrinsic qualities of movements and body shapes. A personalized mask is less remote from dramatic characterization.

Exercises for the Actor Using the Neutral Mask

Most teachers of the mask believe that training should be a *via negativa:* they will not tell the student what to do, but they will point out mistakes after they have been made. "By blocking the path taken by the actor," writes Rolfe, "you oblige him to look for another. . . . Each restriction placed on

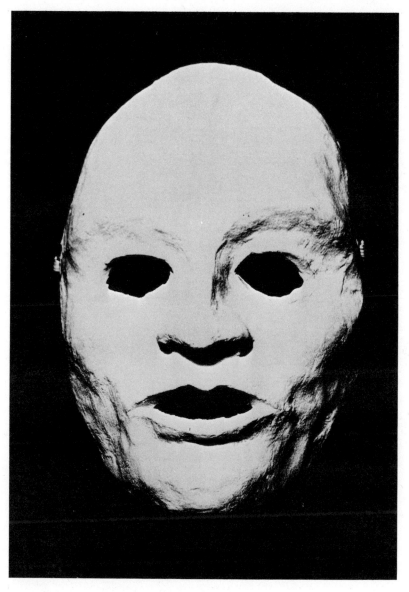

FIGURE 2. *The Andrew Hepburn mask*

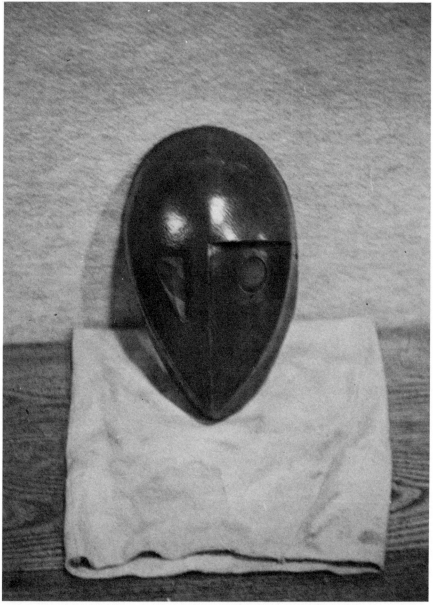

FIGURE 3. *Carlo Mazzone-Clementi's metaphysical mask*

the actor forces his imagination to seek ways to get around it."[11] The teacher cannot provide a model or a set of rules. The student must look for the condition of neutrality within himself. Since bodies are unique, each person's neutrality is his own: there is no single pattern. Hayes-Marshall says that "if a student's work creates fire, I'm not interested in saying it's not fire." Yet in the pursuit of neutrality, a lapse into psychology is perceived as an error. To see such lapses, and to train his students to see them, the teacher must have experienced them in himself.

A period of training, often as long as a year, is required before students attempt the mask. The training period is devoted to acrobatics and conditioning, to developing an awareness of the body's articulations and of the images that the body can project into space. The mask then becomes a way of learning the meaning of those articulations and images.

Most teachers introduce the mask with a talk on its design and significance. Then the actor studies the mask: at the Ecole Lecoq, that study lasts for eight days. The moment of putting on the mask is crucial, since the body will immediately begin to accept or reject the mask. The actor may feel the urge to impose a movement or a body image, but he must inhibit that urge, allowing his own thoughts, his breathing, and his stance to be replaced by those of the mask. Lecoq does not allow his students to view themselves in a mirror at this point, but some teachers find that the mirror can help a student see the change in his condition. The mask is treated with the respect due to a human face. It is handled by the sides or by top and bottom; one never grabs it by the nose or places the hand over its eyes. There is no speaking in the neutral mask; if the student needs to say something, he must first raise the mask onto the forehead.

The first exercises begin from sleep, the most fundamental of resting states.[12] The study of neutrality starts with simple activities such as standing, walking, sitting, or picking up an object, as performed in the mask. The first level of error is gratuitous movement. In walking, one student will bounce, another will sway, another will take extra steps after the forward movement has stopped; one will look at the ceiling, another will look at his feet. In standing, one will scratch his head, another will put his hands on his hips. One student will take hold of an object several times before lifting it, another as he picks it up will make gestures to show how heavy it is. Such movements are imposed on the action; the student must find a way to do the action without them. By making mistakes, however, a student begins to learn how his habits lead him away from neutrality.

A second level of error has to do with the tempo of movement. The actor may seize an object abruptly, without preparation, or he may wait so long that when he picks up the object, the need to do so is gone. Either error will leave questions in an observer's mind. "Why so fast?" Or "why so slow?" If the question arises, the action is not neutral—an attitude has intruded on the movement. There is a moment when the body is ready to move, and if the movement happens at that moment, no question arises.

A third level of error is marked by the imposed attitude. The student performs a single action, but in a manner that creates the image of a character with prior experience of the action. The hands may be so stiff that they seem fearful or hostile. The chest may be sunken, expressing fatigue or cunning, or expanded, showing curiosity. The student must examine his customary self-use, because neutral action is performed as if for the first time. No one part of the body, nor the mask itself, can draw attention; in neutrality, the entire body and the surrounding space are perceived with equal weight. To focus on a part of the space—to expand the chest, for instance—is to be dramatic and not neutral.

The initial exercises introduce the student to a process of experiment, perception, and change. Each error brings discovery of a new approach to the task. The new approach is questioned, in its turn, bringing the student closer to a condition that he can fully achieve only for brief moments. The research of neutrality never ends, for every level of knowledge, if accepted rather than questioned, becomes a technique imposed on the mask. The advantage for the performer is that each new technique is stronger than the old because it is closer to the body's natural functioning.

After exploring simple actions in the mask, the teacher may assign extended scenarios in which the person wearing the mask encounters elements or objects. Some of the common exercises are as follows:

1. The figure wakes and moves toward light;
2. The figure wakes in the desert and walks into a city;
3. The figure wakes in the desert; goes to a river and enters it, perceiving its flow and its source; finds a tree, from which a bird flies;
4. The figure encounters another figure, of the opposite sex (man meets woman);
5. The figure wakes and stands in a fog; explores the fog; finds himself at the edge of the sea, as the fog clears; throws a stone out to sea;
6. The figure walks along a beach; goes to the end of a pier; sees a boat moving across the water, and waves to a person in the boat;
7. The figure walks to the end of the pier and pulls in a sailboat; punts the boat away from the shore, raises sail, and rests at the tiller; lowers sail and throws out the anchor; casts a net and pulls it in full of fish; lifts the anchor, raises sail, and rests at the tiller.

The teacher looks for simplicity and clarity in the actor's imagery. Lecoq has said that "If the Neutral Mask looks at the sea, it becomes the sea." Does the actor accept the environment, or does he establish a dramatic conflict with it? Does he show us the sea, or his own impression of the sea? Are the imaginary objects established in their weight and texture as well as in their shape? Is each experience—touching the earth, entering the river, casting the net—finished before another is begun? Does the actor show awareness of another person, or is he only compelled in a social way to look at him? Does he show awareness of objects and elements, or is he only compelled in an intellectual way to touch them? Is his breathing quiet and regular, or jagged and dramatic? Does the stone continue its flight after it leaves the actor's hand? "How can I discover without curiosity?" protests the student, and in asking the question he defines the assignment.

In the exercise called "Discovery," the actor carrying the mask assumes a position of sleep, while the teacher places around him objects of various shapes, weights, and textures. The assignment is to wake up, to explore several of the objects as if one had no experience of them, and to return to sleep. Familiar objects are treacherous; it is tempting to hold a knife by the handle, to pick up a book and read the print, to open an umbrella, to bounce a ball, but these familiar actions may assume a history of interaction with the object. The neutral mask might discover the working of the umbrella, but only as the result of an exploration; and that discovery, if it comes, has no psychological or intellectual purpose. The mask does not impose a concept on the environment, but accepts the experiences contained within the environment.

Not all neutrality exercises cast the actor as a human figure. Rolfe asks her students to identify with animals in the neutral mask; or to recreate the images of a *haiku*. Hayes-Marshall gives assignments in the elements: earth, air, fire, and water. By asking the student to carry the mask in a non-human image, the teacher extends the student's ability to enter a condition without imposing personal associations on it.

Benefits of the Training for the Actor

The neutral mask is a way of understanding performance, not a way of performing. The mask is a tool for analyzing the quality of the body's action. The mask hides the face, but reveals the attitudes and intentions, the nuances, the feeling tones, that are otherwise only dimly sensed in a person's motion or stillness. When he carries it, the actor must communicate through his whole person; and the spectator must perceive the expression of the whole person. The experience can be frightening, because it is like being, or perceiving, a second person within the familiar body. Because the neutral mask is empty to begin with, it fills with whatever expression is perceived in the body. Hayes-Marshall says that ''a good neutral mask looks like the person who puts it on.'' Trained observers know the expression of the face before the student takes off the mask. The mask draws attention to the body's points of resistance, and demands, as the price of comfort, that the body be integrated in a single image. Carrying the mask is internal and external, analytic and holistic. The dichotomies of physical and emotional technique are united in a single experience. The neutral mask allows the quality of a movement to be seen; it takes that quality on itself and magnifies it.

Because it requires participation in an image different from oneself, the mask attacks mumble-and-scratch naturalism. Peter Frisch has described the kind of actor who says, ''Oh, I know that character, that character is just like me,'' when the truth is that ''the character is nothing like they are. They see it through their own neurotic self-image.''[13] The neutral mask can lead an actor to reject his habitual identifications in favor of a deeper, simpler understanding of his powers of expression.

The neutral mask teaches simplicity in stillness and in activity. When an actor throws a stone, each part of his body should throw the stone, and no part should do anything else. The action should be allowed to complete itself before it is terminated, and it should terminate either in stillness or in the incipience of the next action. Bad movement training confuses activity with commitment; in the hands of a good teacher, the mask shows us that many details of our movement are parasitic behaviors, caused by resistance to the task at hand. When the actor clears himself of habitual assumptions and attitudes, he becomes a finely tuned instrument, capable of recording the subtle phases of perception and intention. An actor who is comfortable in stillness and activity, who commits to both, and who moves easily from one state to the other, is an actor who commands the stage. The neutral mask provides a way for a teacher and student momentarily to grasp and hold on to the intangible quality called "presence."

The actor cannot be neutral; he can only hope to attain moments of neutral action. Yet the pursuit of neutrality purifies him, making his very errors more commanding. Shedding personal cliches and habitual responses, he looks deeper into himself for images that are truly his own. After experiencing the neutral mask, he moves on to expressive masks, to the speaking masks of *commedia,* and finally to the clown nose and the discovery of his personal clown. Beneath these masks, however, is the state of near-neutrality: in a sense, the actor wears the neutral mask beneath every other mask and every other character. Lecoq likens the neutral mask to "the bottom of the sea," whereas "the Expressive Mask is like waves."

The neutral mask is not a way of performing; there is no neutral "style" of acting. The mask helps to identify a resting state for the actor, a condition of presence from which all things are possible, and to which all actions return at completion.

FOOTNOTES

[1] Jacques Copeau, quoted in Elizabeth Shepley Sergeant, "A New French Theatre," *The New Republic* 10 (1917): 351.

[2] Copeau, "Notes on the Actor," trans. Harold J. Salemson, *Actors on Acting,* eds. Toby Cole and Helen Krich Chinoy (New York: Crown Publishers, 1970), p. 220.

[3] Ibid., p. 222.

[5] Etienne Decroux, quoted by Thomas Leabhart in "Etienne Decroux on Masks," *Mime Journal,* no. 2 (1975): 56. Decroux calls the mask "inexpressive" rather than "neutral."

[5] This and subsequent quotations of Lecoq are taken from notes of an interview by Sears Eldredge, trans. Fay Lecoq, in Eldredge, "Masks: Their Use

and Effectiveness in Actor Training Programs'' (Ph.D. diss., Michigan State University, 1975), p. 390.

[6] Interview by Eldredge, op. cit., p. 373. Bari Rolfe is a former student of Lecoq, and has taught neutral mask at the University of Washington and the International Mime Institute.

[7] Rolfe, ''The Mime of Jacques Lecoq,'' *The Drama Review* 16, no. 1 (March 1972): 37.

[8] This and other quotations of Richard Hayes-Marshall are drawn from interviews by Hollis Huston on 26 February and 2 April, 1977. Hayes-Marshall studied and taught at the Ecole Lecoq, and now heads the Hayes-Marshall School of Theatre in Portland, Oregon.

[9] Letter dated 14 March 1977. Hepburn and Richard Nichols studied Lecoq mask theory under Arne Zaslove, and have gone on to teach in American universities. Nichols taught neutral and expressive mask for four years at Ohio State University.

[10] Michel Saint-Denis, *Theatre: Rediscovery of Style* (New York: Theatre Arts Books, 1969), p. 103.

[11] ''The Mime of Jacques Lecoq,'' p. 38.

[12] The exercises described in the following paragraphs are drawn from the practice of Lecoq and of others who have studied with him or whose teachers were influenced by him: Huston, Hayes-Marshall, Nichols, and Rolfe.

[13] From an interview by Eldredge, op. cit., p. 349. Frisch taught mask at Harvard University, though he does not teach neutral mask.

RICHARD NICHOLS *teaches Lecoq-based movement training for actors at the University of Nebraska-Lincoln. He received his Ph.D. from the University of Washington where he studied Lecoq methods under Arne Zaslove. Dr. Nichols is a student of Japanese kendo and iai-do and is an active member of the Asian theatre and theatre movement projects of the American Theatre Association.*

Empty-Handed Combat in the Actor Training Program

by Richard Nichols

WHAT FOLLOWS IS an exploratory analysis of the relationship between actor training in general and empty-handed combat taught within the context of Lecoq-based movement training for actors.[1] The intent here is not to outline the various techniques for staging fight scenes, but rather to draw attention to areas in which empty-handed combat experiences can be of profound value when properly integrated with other elements of the actor's training and education.

As perhaps the least known of the many integrated move-ment techniques employed in contemporary actor training programs, empty-handed combat is difficult to define or to explain. While it shares occasional goals and philosophical bases with some of the martial arts, empty-handed combat is neither - aikido nor *karate*. It bears no resemblance to *kung fu, t'ai chi,* or *tae kwan do*. Empty-handed combat, as the term will be used in the following pages, denotes an integral part of the Lecoq movement training system for actors, and for that reason also is concerned with experiences beyond the technical demands of a fight scene or a given *kata* (form) from one of the many martial arts.

Within the context of my own teaching, combat is taught before mask and mime work, but after students have experienced the conditioning exercises developed by Lecoq to support the actor's movement self-education. Prior to the combat experience, students play a wide range of games to develop trust in others and confidence in themselves; and they receive detailed, intensive instruction in the techniques of delivering and taking punches, slaps, kicks, etc. With six hours a week in class, fifteen students can be prepared for combat techniques in about three weeks. In another three weeks, the rudiments of the various techniques can be taught and the students released to choreograph two-person fight scenes outside of class. While the scenes are prepared in non-class time, it is advantageous to use class time for the introduction of elements related both to the combat work and to acting problems in general: juggling, for example, to develop hand–eye coordination; and basic circus techniques for balance and general body–space awareness.

The students approach the fight scene as they would ap-proach any other scene prepared for the acting studio. A situation is selected and given circumstances determined. Individual intentions (objectives) are clarified and the range of appropriate actions (slaps, punches, etc.) explored and nar-rowed. The goal is a fight scene with a beginning, middle, and

Empty-handed combat is a confrontation: actors with themselves, and actors with the essential elements of the acting process.

end; a scene in which the actor experiences exhaustive, yet controlled, physical activity in union with consistent physical characterization and organic emotional response to the situation, intention, and actions. What is described above realistically can be achieved in seven to eight weeks. In that same amount of time, most other martial arts are still at the level of fundamentals and the art of acting seldom discussed. In contrast, eight weeks of Lecoq-based combat training will give the student an analog to his concerns in the acting studio; he learns techniques that will be of direct benefit in the staging of fight scenes; and he begins the process of movement self-education.

By now it should be clear that empty-handed combat is not intended to foster a new generation of stunt men and women. To repeat, empty-handed combat is an integral element in movement education, one attempting to help each student's body move toward what Lecoq calls the ''neutral'' state. Neutrality does not denote a state of nothingness—it implies instead a physical economy, an active state of ''availability'' (Lecoq's word). It implies an ability to improvise in the actor's changing environment, to respond freely and efficiently to changing internal and external stimuli. In a very real sense the neutral state is the one we would have if we matured without the physical and mental buffetings we all experience, buffetings that shape our bodies and mental outlook. It is a state of open acceptance of what *is,* a condition in which large, unfettered, unconstrained gesture (the word is used in its broadest sense here) is again possible. It also is a goal that is unapproachable without some alteration in our present states of being.

By its very nature, combat deals with primitive emotions and violent physical activity. Women especially—although men are not immune—find a joyous physical and emotional release within the context of the combat experience. They sense that their true physical potential far exceeds the earlier, self-perceived potential. For many students, violence is now for the first time approved behavior, and when full, organic, guttural yelling supports the violence, the student learns a valuable lesson in the relationship of emotion, voice, movement, and the shape of that movement. A reminder: the violence is controlled by technique and the situations are imaginary.

Combat sharpens kinesthetic sensitivity and firms the link between movement and emotion, for the individual movements in combat lead to a heightened sense of space and of the self in that space. Altered kinesthetic perceptions of self are accompanied by changing perceptions of others, for the physical contact demanded in combat requires that actors touch each other—not just with the hands, but with the entire body. And this important lesson in tactile communication is achieved without calling awkward attention to itself. Clearly, the combat experience leads the actor to a more positive appreciation of his body as a communicative instrument. For that reason, combat also addresses itself to the needs of the human being; at the same time it works to foster the physical and emotional development so important to the actor.

The work done by Feldenkrais, Rolfe, and others makes it clear that the body is a walking history of who and what we are. Experiences that mark our passage through life are imprinted in our very muscles. The sum of those experiences, and of our reactions to them, is manifested in the way we move, breathe, behave, and in the way we present ourselves to others. If we imagine the actor's body as a prism, it will be seen as the medium through which the actor's mental image of his or her ideal characterization for a role must be projected in action on the stage. The extent to which the prism is clear determines the ability of the image to pass through with minimal distortion. If the prism is flawed the physical, emotional, and aural images transmitted to the audience will not be those solely of the character intended. Rather, they will be tinged with images of the actor himself; and such flaws often will be present without the actor's knowledge, the result of unconscious mannerisms. Lecoq calls them "parasites."[2]

In many ways these parasites are linked inextricably with the actor's self-image. Every acting teacher is familiar with the student whose self-image is so confined, so protective, that he cannot "see" himself as anyone but himself. Moshe Feldenkrais notes that the manner in which we carry/present ourselves is based on our self-image; an image which may differ from reality by 300 percent or more.[3] Because habitual movement patterns are an integral part of any self-image, any long-term alteration in that image is unlikely until new patterns are experienced and subsequently substituted for old ones.

Empty-handed combat can be of immense value in the breaking up of old, established movement patterns: the physical extremities demanded in combat can lead the student away from usual movement/behavior patterns. Once these patterns are altered, "it is easier to effect changes in thinking and feeling, for the muscular part through which thinking and feeling reach our consciousness has changed."[4] In conjunction with exercises to reinforce pattern changes, empty-handed combat can serve as one means of reducing parasites at the same time that it leads the actor to a more positive view of his emotional and physical capabilities—present and potential.

Aikido, t'ai chi, and other martial forms mentioned at the outset of this discussion seek inner harmony and, by extension, the amelioration of problems with self-image. The union of balance, economy of effort, mental tranquility, and respiration as the source of energy is used to bring about the desired coordination of mind and body. Each martial art has undeniable value for the given indifidual, and the presence of martial arts in training programs should be maintained wherever possible. At the same time, however, teachers and students should not forget that the needs of the actor and the needs of the martial arts enthusiast are not necessarily identical. The martial arts were developed for fighting—either from an offensive or defensive stance—and not for the needs of actors. It can be difficult for the young actor to apply the subtle lessons of *t'ai chi* patterns ("Needle at Sea Bottom," for example) to the problems faced in playing Hedda Gabler or Hamlet. Too frequently, those who teach the forms do not understand, or cannot establish, the connection between a given martial art and the problems facing an actor as he approaches a role. When no consideration is given to the actor's craft, there is no reinforcement of lessons learned in the acting studio, and, in that regard, the movement training is less than it should be. All martial arts have the potential to make a direct contribution (narrow though it may be) to the actor's craft, but teachers must do a better job of clarifying those contributions and their applications. The advantage of Lecoq-based combat is that it encompasses nearly all the goals of martial arts training at the same time it actively involves the actor in the imaginative processes and physical craft of acting.

With the actor's needs in mind, let us look at various aspects of the Lecoq-based combat experience:

1. *The presence of character intentions.* Each participant wants to defeat his opponent, to inflict pain, to smash in his face (I am referring to character intentions, of course). The simplicity, the directness, of the chosen intentions helps the young actor better understand the importance of intentions as a source of action and connected emotional response.

2. *Selection of appropriate actions.* One of the most difficult lessons for young actors is the selection of the appropriate physical response once the intention is selected. Faced with the problems inherent in the creation of any unscripted work, the student combatant quickly senses that there is an infinite number of actions appropriate for a given intention. By this time, however, the student already has had opportunities to explore the interplay of movement effort, shape, timing, and emotional key and begins to narrow the range of possible actions. "Is the physical activity appropriate to the character's needs and the situation at this particular moment?" That question is continually asked during the development of the fight scene and there are few students who do not discern the connection between their work on the fight scene and their work on a scene for the acting studio.

3. *Committed physical and emotional responses to the situation.* Combat, and honesty in any other scene work as well, cannot exist without full physical and emotional commitment from both partners. Students learn that there can be no halfway in their giving of themselves on the stage. At the same time, however, they also learn the difference between enthusiastic, uncontrolled response and focused, efficient expenditure of physical and emotional energy.

4. *Acceptance of the imagined situation in which the fight is contained.* Both partners must establish clear characterizations, complete with detailed given circumstances (furniture, props, and other accoutrements should be imaginary, not actual) and behavior consistent with the level of theatricality established at the scene's outset. In short, both actors must behave *as if* they are involved in actual weaponless combat. Without full acceptance of the characters and situation, the combat becomes a mere exercise in movement activity.

5. *The need for mental images, focused outside the actor.* There is a marked similarity between athletes and actors; both must deal with images. High jumpers and pole vaulters, for example, are known for their ability to project a mental image to a point in space and to physically identify with that image. Before each jump the athlete imagines himself moving through space, approaching the bar, lifting, and clearing. He sees and feels himself moving from point A to point B, and he strives for a physical union with the imagined action.

The actor involved in combat also must employ such mental activity as he imagines his hand, foot, or knee moving through space to stop at the envisioned location. Although the punch to the stomach, for example, stops at an envisioned spot one-quarter of an inch inside the abdomen wall, the actor's safety is a primary concern; therefore, blows do not usually touch the person for whom they are intended. Thus, the image takes on even greater importance because slaps and other movements pass within a fraction of an inch of an opponent's face. The fight techniques are too complex to be outlined in this discussion, but there is an appearance of true contact, even in the arena situation. Without the projection of such images, fidelity is not possible. The mental discipline encountered in the use of images in combat enhances the actor's ability to see imaginary objects or people in space. The value to the actor playing Macbeth in the banquet scene is clear indeed.

6. *Development of kinesthetic sensitivity and the ability to improvise in space.* The basketball player, to return to my comparison of actor and athlete, is a model of kinesthetic awareness as he or she moves up and down the court. On the fast-break, the man with the ball is attempting to mentally out-imagine his opponent, laying out possibilities for future action as he proceeds down the court. Kinesthetically, he also is sensing subtle alterations in the space relationships around him. While he may have a range of possible movements in mind, he must improvise as the changing situation demands. He must play the moment. The actor involved in the fight scene must do likewise.

Detailed rehearsals lead to the scene itself, but at any moment the rehearsal or the performance may not go as planned. The changing configurations of bodies in space, especially in falls and rolls, demand that the actor develop a circle of awareness, a full 360 degrees. Without such awareness, it is difficult for the student to play the moment as required; to improvise in order to maintain control of the scene under duress. The lessons learned from combat can be a positive factor in the creation of an ensemble and the development of a sensitivity to the flow of crowd scenes.

7. *A continual movement toward "other consciousness."* Combat requires intense concentration, focused on one's partner. Each combatant must move out of himself and direct his energy out and to his partner. Stanislavski refers to this phenomenon as "infecting" one's partner, and combat can be an excellent device for demonstrating the ebb and flow of energy on stage, especially when that rhythm is based on the interplay between violently opposed intentions.

8. *An understanding of the importance of "phrasing."* Young actors often strive for a given effect without going through all the steps necessary to achieve it. Empty-handed combat teaches actors to do one thing at a time, giving each action a beginning, middle, and an end. To throw a punch while a slap is not yet complete can be dangerous as well as theatrically ineffective. The stress upon one thing at a time has a salutary influence on scene work, not only because it teaches clarity of gesture and related physical activity, but also because it places a premium on the ability to stay in the moment, playing one beat at a time.

9. *Development of physical efficiency through exercises preparatory to the combat experience and through an understanding of the flow of effort.* The physical education which is at the heart of the Lecoq technique is founded, to a large extent, on the rediscovery of (and growing sensitivity to) one's own rhythms and effort patterns. Students gradually sense the importance of respiration in all movement patterns, and close attention is given to the very way in which students view movement itself. Many students—far too many—have developed mental sets that result in inefficient movement patterns and expenditure of immense, uncontrolled energy when they encounter any exercise calling for large muscle activity. The combat experience quickly demonstrates the need for efficiency; without it, students have difficulty completing the fight scene. More importantly, combat brings the realization that effort is a complex sequence: mental preparation for each action, the decision to act, the action itself, the subsiding and cessation of effort, a moment of rest, an evaluation of the results of the action, and a new cycle of activity based on the information gleaned from the preceding cycle. Certainly, this flow is nearly instantaneous in many cases, but a study of the flow can bring new depth to the actor's work in the acting studio, especially once he realizes that his own flow of effort may need to be altered in order to more accurately reflect the effort patterns of the character at hand.

10. *Maintenance of Stanislavski's "two perspectives of a role."* The physical and emotional stretching that occurs in the context of empty-handed combat is a vivid object lesson in the importance of control—of technique—in the actor's craft. No matter how intense the activity and the emotion, the actor must learn to develop a center of calm. Martial arts advocates call the process "centering." At stake is the nurturing of two necessary perspectives: that of the character being played; and that of the actor himself as he looks at the character, at himself, and at the changing environment in which he works.

11. *An appreciation for discipline as the source of freedom.* This aspect of the work is suggested in each of the preceding elements, but it deserves consideration on its own merits. Despite the emphasis placed on safety, there is always an element of danger in the combat experience, and students are quick to appreciate that danger. At the same time, however they also develop a healthy respect for discipline as the key to their continued well-being. Out of the maturing discipline comes trust in one's partner (availability) and confidence in oneself (commitment). The students sense the positive, supportive side of discipline in their chosen craft. Rather than viewing discipline as a fetter, they understand that it truly is one key to the continuing development of physical ease, physical efficiency, and a freer, more organic emotional response to the imagined world at hand.

In sum, Lecoq-based combat training represents a microcosm of the acting process itself. The actor must define the who, what, where, and when. He must play an intention with full commitment to the situation and the actions required. The intentions and actions must be shaped by clearly delineated given circumstances and integrated with an organic emotional response to the character's needs and actions within the imagined situation. Emotions must be balanced by intense concentration and superb physical technique in the delivery of each and every blow. When confidence in oneself and trust in one's partner are added to the above elements, we have the ingredients of an experience that can bring unique rewards to the student actor at the same time that it serves as a means of movement self-education for the student as human being.

FOOTNOTES

[1] I use the phrase "Lecoq-based" for two reasons. First, I have not studied with Jacques Lecoq. My training was received under the tutelage of Arne Zaslove, whose influence is manifest in this article and whose reputation as a master teacher must be acknowledged. Second, my approach to movement training incorporates elements from other sources, most notably the work of Moshe Feldenkrais and my own training in Japanese classical theatre and *iaido* (swordsmanship).

[2] There are many other terms for these mannerisms. Rudolf Laban, for example, calls them "unconscious gesture." See *Mastery of Movement*, 3d ed., revised by Lisa Ullman.

[3] Self-image, and the alteration of it, is a central concern in the work of Moshe Feldenkrais. Read the opening chapters of his *Awareness through Movement: Health Exercises for Personal Growth* (New York: Harper and Row, 1972).

[4] Feldenkrais, *Awareness through Movement*, p. 9.

VALENTINA LITVINOFF *works with actors, dancers, and musicians in her New York studio; conducts workshops and seminars at universities; lectures, writes, and choreographs. Among the New York theatre productions for which she has done choreography are* The Madwoman of Chaillot, Dark of the Moon, Salem Story, *and Euripides'* Trojan Women, *in which she also performed. She has taught, lectured or choreographed at Pratt Institute, University of North Carolina, Ohio University, Pennsylvania State University, University of San Jose, and Naropa Institute, among others. A scholarship graduate of the Neighborhood Playhouse Studios, she has studied modern dance, ballet, and a number of ethnic dance forms, and has worked with Martha Graham, Doris Humphrey, and Louis Horst. Her studies in the use of self include the Alexander Technique, the Todd-Sweigard method, and Charlotte Selver's Sensory Awareness. Ms. Litvinoff co-chairs the Project on Studies in Human Movement for the American Dance Guild. She is the author of* The Use of Stanislavsky Within Modern Dance, *and has published articles in* The Drama Review, The Journal of Aesthetic Education, Dance Scope, Dance Magazine, The Journal of Aesthetics and Art Criticism, *and* Monograph One *of the Congress on Research in Dance.*

The Natural and the Stylized: In Conflict or Harmony?

by Valentina Litvinoff

AN AXIOM HAS EMERGED out of my explorations and work in movement for theatre, dance, daily living, and in the use of self for music. According to the axiom, three conditions must be compatible if an individual's movement is to function well: (1) *the needs of the human organism,* (2) *the claims of the activity* of the moment, and (3) *the demands of the environment.* When the three necessities are not divergent but mutually supportive and benevolent, that is, when the individual gives his own organism its due in the process of moving and when the demands of the task as well as conditions of the environment also mesh sympathetically, then movement may be perceived to "work." The axiomatic interdependence of the three entities concerns both the actor's movement on the stage as well as human movement in general.

The needs of the organism are those elusive interconnections composed of breathing, of the dynamic relationships of body segments in their response to gravitational pull, muscular tonus, and distribution of ongoing energies throughout the self; in short, that multitude of somatic occurrences that go under the general heading of "organismic functioning."

The claims of an activity could involve numberless accommodations. They are what Charlotte Selver, quoting her teacher Elsa Gindler, used to summarize by saying, "What does it want from me?" The claims of an activity compose an area studied by Effort–Shape (originated by Rudolf Laban) in an ordered observation of types of energy and qualities of movement which particular tasks call for. When a person shows a well-functioning response to the demands of an activity, usually "efficiency of movement"—kinesiologists' favorite reference—is intrinsically mixed up with spontaneity. What we are talking about is a caliber of reactivity. But to understand the term reactivity on a more complex level we need to recall that actors' work adds another dimension to the link between the individual and the activity at hand: as soon as the individual appears within the framework of the theatre, the activity becomes one of judiciously selected movement—even when a lot of it is improvised on the spot. The activity, of course, can be obedient to conventions of a particular movement scheme or form. But even at its most naturalistic, an actor's staged chopping of wood is, as we recognize, quite different from his own action of chopping at a real campfire site. The problem then becomes one of reconciling this contradiction: how can stylizations, simplifications, and distortions (whether in "far-out" theatre or the "near" real) be brought into congruence with the human demands of the actor's own human nature, rather than being an imposition upon it? Only in the reconciliation of the two opposites, the natural self of the actor and stylizations of theatre, can the actor's movement on the stage be convincing. In this welding into a unity of an imposed movement pattern and the actor's own guts, the actor's creativity is stimulated. A sense of spontaneous freedom arises, issuing from the experiential recognition of two basic necessities: the needs of the organism and the claims of the activity or of the form.

The welding I speak of does not happen in a vacuum. Until the demands of the environment are also recognized and absorbed, the harmony within the trinity of requirements is not complete. This third element is much less susceptible to the actor's conscious control that the other two, the needs of the organism and the claims of the activity of the moment.

In a larger sense, the whole dynamic of a society is the environment, for the social fabric impinges in some way upon the labor of the actor as artist and as human being. Can a society which has been so invariably characterized by the words "alienation," "fragmentation," "anxiety," and "fear" not make its mark upon the way we move? Our ways in the use of self, in relating to gravity, in allowing energies and qualities of movement appropriate to activity are intimately conditioned by our common time and place. Yet the effects of today's dominant recidivous influences are not inevitable. Just as many of us refuse to be alienated from each other, we can also refuse to be alienated from our own bodies. Moreover, we can reject the separation of organismic movement from the demands of style. A receptivity to the currents of humanism which struggle for an increasing influence within our society and lives can have a positive reflection within our wholistic self and in our use of self in theatre.

A more spotlighted view of the demands of the environment focuses upon the playing area, compeers, and immediate surroundings (actual or imaginary) pertinent to the production.

This view encourages an awareness of the entire work of movement in the production rather than of "my" movement alone. When the individual is open to the environment, "my" movement is never an isolated solo; not even on an empty stage where I stand alone. The solo becomes more eloquent for its invisible connectedness.

This statement of philosophy, then, is derived from and contributes to the content and the methodology of my work in movement for the theatre. But before attempting to describe a few procedures of this work it is necessary to qualify more specifically the aims of movement training.

Aims of Movement Training

Movement training must provide the actor with the means for finding and developing whatever is needed in movement for *any* production, *any* style or character.

No strange style, whether avant-garde or obscure historical, will long puzzle the actor who is in touch with a methodology for finding the essence of the needed movement. Having found the essence, it is a challenging but not difficult task to develop this beginning and to live in this movement—to breathe with it and to speak with ease, to feel an availability, a fulfillment, a physical logic.

The procedure for this type of accomplishment unfolds in several ways. A particular mode of movement for a particular production may involve distortions, stylizations, and "extended" uses of self. To become capable of invoking such magnifications the actor must have many full experiences of two types.

The first is the use of self as a human being in organismic balance. This means a shedding of hindrances: rigidities, flabbinesses, misalignments, and mannerisms. The aim is to free the body, and the process within the work I am discussing is multifaceted, inclusive of structured and unstructured exercises, improvisations, and experiments. A dominant feature of the process is its synthesis of a number of studies in body education. The Alexander Technique, Todd–Sweigard "ideokinesis," and Selver's Awareness are among major influences within our work.[1] (Here, and in subsequent pages, the words "our" and "we" refer to the work of my students and myself.) The creative synthesis of Alexander, Sweigard, and Selver is an important and distinguishing feature in the implementation of our aims.

The second type of movement experience necessary for the actor is the extension of his improved use of self as a human being to meet the demands of the theatre. Now the better integrated student experiences many qualities of motion, diverse rhythmicities, and movement skills. He develops a repertoire of more complex coordinations through a number of means, all natural and unforced while being increasingly challenging. Strength, flexibility, and endurance are promoted through special techniques. Kinesthetic awareness becomes sharpened; a most productive study I call "breath-supportedness" in movement is discovered. Imagination and creativity are stimulated. The performer learns how to approach the study of styles. The work is neuropsychophysical in all its aspects.

Within the framework of the two parts of this process exercises and explorations are developed for particular objectives, and a generous use is made of heritage in movement and dance. A form of T'ai Chi, patterns of Spanish dance, Yoga exercises, the Japanese theatre walk, selected modern dance progressions, the combination of movement and voice are all utilized to make the more fully integrated human being a well-tuned instrument for the theatre. The usages are employed not mechanically but in meaningful service of the process.

We all surely note that this day is an era of many body techniques. Valid and useful as numbers of the approaches are, the decisive element is less in the content of a discipline than in the use a discipline is put to in the context of theatre training aims. Besides, a particular discipline (assuming it is taught in a way which relates it directly to the several species of theatre proliferating now) may be presented to participants at an inappropriate point in their development. For example, a few years ago I had the pleasure of spending a semester teaching movement at a university theatre department where previous training had consisted only of courses in mime. Unquestionably an important theatrical technique, this work nevertheless had produced among the students an unbalanced use of self. Obviously the students had studied particular stylizations and conventions too early and, as a result, emerged with well-learned patterns which dominated much of what they tried to do, regardless of the patterns' fitness to the task. What is the benefit of this type of acquisition of a style, if mannerisms are thereby acquired unconsciously as a kind of conditioning, imprinted upon the students' limited coordinations? Yet, had the mime training been preceded by the study of basics in human movement, as well as by the experiencing of a number of motor qualities, the conventions of mime would perhaps have been understood in their context as a specific technique, instead of being absorbed as the epitome of movement. What could have been valuable training in a theatre style proved instead to be a superficial veneer laid over a range of bad physical habits, usages long in need of correction.

Possibly the most significant part of our work is that the actor emerges able to find ways of movement appropriate for whatever new problems are encountered, and able to make a selective search for cues for the needed movement. Cues are discovered in the production or project itself as well as in art and cultural artifacts related to it. Moreover, a particular use of the Method of Physical Action, based on Stanislavsky's innovation, becomes instrumental in finding a type of movement.[2]

I use the terms *physical action* and *physical motivation* interchangeably to denote an impelling physical impulse within a movement. My arm is being lifted, for example, in order *to bring it up;* or it is being initially lifted *to bring it down;* it is being lifted *to reach toward you;* or it is being lifted for me *to sense the movement.* The patterning of the arm movement is almost identical in all the examples, but the impelling inner action is different in each case. Therefore the coloration of the movement also differs. The potentials of the impelling motor are multitudinous. A physical motivation may be supportive of an activity or in opposition to it, depriving the activity of fruition; one physical action may be frustrated by a conflicting physical action; or, more than one contrasting physical action may divide the body. These approaches could result in telling stylizations. Variations upon this theme of physical action reverberate with theatrical complexities. (Understand, I am not talking about "acting out" a particular quality or manner but about the inner physical motor which is the actor's trade secret. In qualifying movement, the physical action is not necessarily acted out. However, at a certain time in the work we study techniques of projecting movement on the stage—an exploration outside the limits of this essay.) The motor within movement, while being "purely" physical, carries an associative train into areas of space, time, and qualities of energy.

In the following descriptions I want to indicate only the simpler phases of how the Physical Action, the Alexander Technique, and the Sweigard approach become integrated in work on alignment, in doing exercises and other sequences, as well as in the development of the actor's stylistic range.

Alignment and the Use of Self

In the process of work on an aspect of alignment, the instructor might ask the students to put the following inner physical action into the body: to permit the shoulder blades to slide down the back. The purpose, to relieve the strain in the upper thoracic area and encourage a better organization of the shoulder girdle. Students simply stand, eyes closed, and exercise the imagination only, making no attempt to "help" physically. After a while another inner physical action may be suggested: to permit the shoulder area, the upper chest, and the thickness of the body in between the front and the back to widen out to the side. The widening begins at the spine and at the sternum and is, at first, done one side at a time. In the student's mind, that area as he perceives it changes shape in the direction of width. The directive to widen is, of course, a classic Alexander usage; the instructor's aware and trained hands may be placed upon the student's shoulder blade area to extend the results of the student's own thinking. This delicate touch, it must be noted, is as educated as it is nonmanipulative. When afterwards the student is asked merely to sense whether there is any difference in the side "worked" with and the other, he invariably expresses a genuine experience of change. These subjective expressions are more important in terms of the student's development than even the visible change which the surprised observer notices.

Combined with thinking directed along a particular physical action, the suggestive power of touch by even the students' inexperienced hands, if their hands are sensitive, can also be productive. As partners, one allows the head "to separate itself from the neck, to go ceiling-ward" while the other, with a butterfly-soft touch, places the right hand at the partner's occipital joint area, the left under the chin. At first I had hesitated to introduce this departure from the orthodox in having the students assist each other, but came to invoke this and other useful variations on Alexander through the inspiration of my earlier study of Sensory Awareness with Charlotte Selver.

It should be noted here that on the occasions when Selver uses touch, her way differs in purpose (and therefore in quality) from touch in Alexander. Selver touches to stimulate the organism's own tendency toward better equilibrium. In some people, the need of the moment may be to release, to relax. In others, it could be to awaken. When the "toucher" is sufficiently aware and sensitive, the quality (firmness, gentleness, placement, movement, tempo, etc.) of what he does initiates a stimulation of the organism in its own functioning. The Alexander touch, by contrast, initiates nothing. It patiently awaits a sign that the receiver's thinking has been registered through the central nervous system, that the intricate chain of neurophysiological messages and feedbacks is activated; then—knowledgeably—the touch softly moves the bones in particular ways in particular directions, extending into movement the new orientations sparked by the individual's thinking.

With an integration of the two modes, the knowing when (and how, and to what end) to use each type of touch is at the base of any physical contact with the students. The work's propelling principle, however, is the imagined physical action. Do we want to lengthen the spine? (Always desirable!) First, employ the magic "as if": from the seventh cervical vertebra hangs a chain, its links observed in our imagination. Inner physical action: to let the chain become heavy, to see it hanging beyond the end of the spine, down to the floor. This image will be recognized from the Todd–Sweigard work. Lulu Sweigard's method, that of kinesiologist and consummate scholar, presents a series of images, developed under laboratory conditions and tested for their efficacy. But—if one knows what one is doing—images may be made to order; the order being the perceived needs of the students. Imagined physical action: to permit my legs to hang in front of the body, from the thigh joints; then, to let my feet make make-believe footprints as I walk; then, to permit my weight to become more fully balanced on my feet. The last may be accomplished through the magic "as if": the buttocks are heaps of heavy molasses sliding down the backs of the legs.

The validity of harnessing the imagination to the faculty of vision for inducing favorable changes in the use of self has been documented by scholars, among them Fritz Popken, who speaks on behalf of the late Dr. Sweigard's work.[3] Ethologist Nikolaas Tinbergen and Wilfred Barlow, M.D., call attention to the phenomenon of directed envisioning within the Alexander Technique.[4] Supportive evidence for both modalities also comes, even if unwittingly, from Pavel W. Simonov in an article published a few years ago in a European theatre journal.

Simonov, a physician and researcher in neurophysiology, summons the authority of contemporary biology and neurophysiology to support Stanislavsky's practices in the Method of Physical Action. "The formation of an image . . .," Simonov points out, "mobilizes the whole many leveled structure" of the actor's nervous system.[5]

Clarity and concreteness of the imagined object and the imagined movement become a tool: as in Simonov-Stanislavsky's *ideomotoric* action, so in Sweigard's *ideokinesis* and in the intensely pursued but somewhat more abstract *directions of movement* in the Alexander Technique. Shall we indulge in the fantasy that upon some celestial happy hunting ground—reserved for the most significant hunters for truth—Stanislavsky, Alexander, and Sweigard are finally talking with one another about the potentials for commonality in the work of all three?

Nonetheless, while the concepts of alignment that form the practice of classical Alexander Technique and the precise images characterizing ideokinesis frequently complement each other, this does not certify complete agreement of the two approaches in interpretation of somatic priorities or in methodology for promoting change. Differences and mutualities cannot be discussed here; enough to say that to plunge into the frequently divergent currents both of interpretation and practice in body education will bring new insights and discoveries. These combine with the substance of one's whole work. The discoveries may be implemented within movement, exercises, and improvisations; such implementation is out of the scope in Alexander, Selver, or Sweigard.

Development Within Movement Themes

Now to illustrate a very simple practice of basics we've been considering: in the process of pursuing one physical action—to let the skin of the footsoles explore the floor while walking about the studio, for example—make a change. The change should happen at a stage of heightened awareness. The physical action now becomes: to make the rest of me be alive to the work of the feet. Presently the whole self is involved in an improvisation which stems from the increasingly aware and therefore more adept use of feet and legs. As the instructor observes the proceedings, further changes in physical action may be suggested depending on what aspects of the procedure need strengthening: to become aware of the shapes I am making in space, to permit my movement to become simple and slow enough so that nothing escapes my awareness, to find out how much space exists between the top of my head and the ceiling. Should the actor find that he is beginning to evolve a rhythmic pattern as he moves, he may decide on the physical action: to strengthen my song.

When a particular orientation has become familiar to the students—as, for example, the experience of freeing the head "out of the body"—an improvisation can extend this orientation further into movement. *To let the top of the head lead me in movement* may become the physical action; and a miner's light on top of his cap, the magic "as if." The students make circles or other designs with the light, permitting increasing participation of the whole self. Recently, in another improvisation, we explored the use and range of the hands by making air murals as large as the studio room. This involved magnitude of movement, changes of level, swooping runs, circling falls.

Obviously, such improvisations teach more than the use of particular alignment orientations within movement. In the air mural the students experienced the complex coordination of a long, slow incised arm motion while feet simultaneously beat a fast staccato with running steps and the torso leaned, twisted, stretched, or bent. Phrasing, coordination, and the unity of parts within the whole were all explored.

Clearly, work on alignment is a dynamic process which easily becomes part of other exercises and projects and need not be confined to a separate frame of reference.

This interpenetrativeness of purposes and of effects, incidentally, typifies our approach in all aspects of work. In doing an exercise of a purely motor type—as in shaping, in stretching, in hanging—are we not also trying expressive possibilities? Are we not also learning something about rhythmicity? In performing a *plié* are we not also touching upon a stylistic convention?

Physical Action in Exercises

In exploring qualities of movement—for example, the quality of swing, rebound, and momentum within the exercise we call the "body swing"—we may invoke diverse physical actions which make subtle differences in the feel of the familiar exercise. New physical actions thus reveal new aspects of movement. *To permit full indenting in and opening out at the thigh joint* makes a particular element of the exercise more vivid. When, however, the physical action is: to permit the momentum to move me, another aspect of the body swing is dominant and activity at the thigh joint becomes secondary, a sort of by-product of the swinging.

The evocation of diverse inner physical actions is an antidote to mechanical repetition and refreshes familiar exercises. In an exercise to increase the range of the legs—"brushes" across the floor—we have customarily given the physical action as: to brace against the floor with the supporting leg. Now, another inner action becomes operative: to get there, to cover space! Inevitably, the quality of the movement becomes more vigorous, with a sense of attack; the tempo is increased, with a sense of urgency. The teacher may indicate a new directive— now the physical action is: to caress the floor—and another stream of consequences is initiated.

We are dealing with inner subtleties of movement. We begin to understand how it is that the emotional and the psychological states of the actor follow the physical "doing." Soon we also find that an empathetic physical action need not

Photo: Susan Katz

FIGURE 1. *Arresting the momentum of a swinging motion, Valentina Litvinoff and students*

be designed into the activity. A slow, sustained movement is one thing when the inner action supports this quality and quite a different thing when the inner imperative is: to bounce!

By what criteria are exercises (structured and unstructured) chosen or invented? The primary aim of an exercise aside (whether to train for endurance, slowness, speed, or to inspire creative teamwork in movement), the exercise must directly evoke certain vital coordinations. It must do so actively, sometimes strenuously. A few of these coordinations have been broached in the use of self and alignment; another instance could be the important mobilization of the iliopsoas group as it connects with the leg muscles. Elusive, difficult to grasp; its implementation, subtle; finally, as effortless as sensory experience, this muscular coordination was prominent in the work of Isadora Duncan. Appropriate implementation of the iliopsoas can be similarly observed in the tiny hops and knee lifts of Pueblo Indian dances; within the large, slow sweep of Chinese stage movement; in the classic movement of Balinese dance; in many folk forms; and in the skipping of a child as yet unschooled in dance. Mere imitation of these and other examples of well defined usage cannot be as helpful to us in the job of learning as are the special exercises and experiments devised within our work for the absorption of this action. As often happens with other aspects of movement, when the iliopsoas coordination has become a purely physical, unstyled experience, it can be implemented more successfully and appreciatively within a particular form.[6] Exercises should at first be simple and logic the of their physical action must be clear for the student. Any complexities and elaborations must arise out of a natural development within the fundamental structure. Experience with valid exercises and usages early in the training will stand the actor in good stead later when playing in period or other styles he confronts what may seem imposed, even grotesque modes. He will then be able to base outward manners upon sound inner psychophysical orientations.

Work on sensing, on comprehending placement as a dynamic process, and on the evocation of basic principles within movement—rather than obedience to rules—animates our procedures. We want to instill movement habits which are as varied and pliable as they are healthy. We want to develop a know-how for creating new patternings and habits. We want to cultivate great plasticity of the nervous system necessary for the quick assimilation of patternings and for the varying rhythmicities of theatre. Thus we work to augment both the experience and the knowledge of potentials of movement.

The stimulus for discovery is ever present for the students. Among their continued discoveries is that consciousness (awareness, sensing) does away with self-consciousness. This kind of experience is a step toward that combination of discipline and spontaneity that is the mark of a well trained actor.

In striving for economy, directness, and the freeing of the body, appropriate physical action leads to the eventual experiencing of these attributes within a huge range of dynamics, from the very subtle to the big and strenuous, from sustained to disjointed or stopped movement. Skill in coordinating speech, voice, and movement is evolved through special approaches. A number of specific stage techniques are studied, such as stage falls, rolling down stairs, carrying people, fighting, and kissing on the stage.

Movement Heritage

It has been mentioned earlier that use is made of our movement and dance heritage. This is done with an awareness of the role a particular form is to play within the aims of actor training. Take T'ai Chi Chuan. Its values for theatre training have been well described, particularly by Sophia Delza.[7] For years T'ai Chi has been one of my devotions. However, having studied both the Wu and the Yang forms, I teach neither. The primary reason is that the learning and the practice of the long, complex form demands its own time; and the time for the actor's training would become disproportionately allotted. Areas of movement which are equally important would receive inadequate attention. Yet T'ai Chi, primarily for its instilling the sensibility of slowness as an organic development, should be included in movement training. The solution for me lies in a form of T'ai Chi almost unknown in the United States. It is composed of a series of short motifs, each repeatable as often or as seldom as one wishes at a particular session.[8] The motifs—all deeply typical of T'ai Chi principles—are aptly suited for inclusion in the whole work of movement training because their number and the amount of time which need be devoted to their practice may be easily varied according to the group's needs and the projects at hand. One of the virtues of these patterns is that they very directly involve particular coordinations which movement training should instill. Among the few contemporary techniques that succeed as well in this regard are the Fundamentals developed by Irmgard Bartenieff of Dance Notation Bureau in New York and Moshe Feldenkrais' work.

As T'ai Chi is used for its own values, other ethnic movement and dance forms are also touched upon for specific ends. The Spanish *Panaderos* has been presented to several groups for its speed, preciseness, inimitable orchestration of the movement of torso, arms, and feet, and for the stylistic perspectives it conveys. When a Spanish sequence is examined for its inferences, it provides the very cues needed for the playing of Lorca. A proliferation of ethnic material is not necessary for the actor's work on style. Worlds are opened by the telling details of a single European folk dance or the Japanese basic theatre walk. If we have been discovering the natural, we now discover that the natural may change into the stylized. In the process, attributes of the natural will not be lost if their absorption by the actors has been pervasive. Rather, the attributes of the natural, appearing in new guises, may be strengthened.

Perhaps it is pertinent to recall now the tripartite axiom mentioned at the beginning of this essay: *the needs of the human organism* are encountered in the practices of the studies indicated, particularly in the work on alignment and the use of self; *the claims of the activity* of the moment are discovered especially through the mobilization of the physical action propelling the activity; the effect of the practices in our work is to bring into greater harmony *the needs of the human organism* and *the claims of the activity* of the moment.

The extent to which we succeed in so doing depends in part upon the third component of the axiom: *the demands of the environment.* When social conditions and human affairs are positive and humane, the practices of our work tend to accord with them receptively and supportively. When, on the contrary, societal environment is reactionary and negative, the practices of our work offer an ameliorative influence.

Styles, Exaggerations, Conventions

In subsequent stages of the work, we find differing meanings of the term environment; we are brought to varied environmental situations, for we now devote considerable concentration to searches in style. And a particular style, of course, issues out of a nurturing geography and cultural milieu. The processes have already dealt to a degree with heightened, selected, changed, or unusual ways of moving. Our many forays to taste various qualities of movement, and the occasional study of an ethnic form, have already encroached upon extended uses of self. Now, however, in a more focused way, usages are devised to prepare the actor for historical styles, for assimilating unusual or obscure styles, and for developing original styles in movement.

As we get into the specifics of period and ethnic styles, we make another profound discovery: the closer we come to fulfilling the demands of a style (both in gross characteristics and in its subtle nuances), the more fully we also meet the demands of studies in human movement and the use of self. The stylized now expresses the natural.

Some illustrations are in order. When a class of actors wanted to find movement for playing Chekhov we utilized as a stylistic cue a legato Russian polka with the typical expansive arm motion. The simple step gave us a generic, cultural background as a basis for the diverse movement of the characters.

Another time, the cast of Euripides' *Trojan Women* faced the problem of achieving the necessary style while developing the agility needed to move upon a complex set of platforms. We began with the platforms. The intent was to explore this environment in ordinary, natural ways of locomotion. Through walking upon the platforms, sitting, lying, making transitory movements between the sitting, rising, or climbing, eventually striding and falling, rolling from one level to another, our coordinations and reflexes became increasingly in tune with the environment. Then it became possible to negotiate the tricky levels of the platforms while using voice, while turning the torso and glance in a direction opposite to the one in which we were going; we were able to run, to stop suddenly, and to do it all fully, freely. We were thus mobilizing our potential for movement within a particular environment. And lo and behold—we found that we *had* the style! It was arrived at indirectly; it issued from our work of connecting our organismic functioning, our human endowment, with the environment.

FIGURE 2. *Sensitivity of the hands may begin an improvisation*

Photo: Susan Katz

A group was once working on an experimental sketch in super slow time. Monotony threatened. The scene was saved from being a static, heavy picture by the actors' practice of T'ai Chi and its organic slowness. No, the piece was not played in T'ai Chi style, but the ability to justify the scene's distended tempo by the sensibility of physically living within the tempo emerged out of the actors' experience in T'ai Chi.

In the course of my residency at the University of North Carolina, we used evocative costumes as well as bits of drapery, a fan, and lace gloves for their suggestion of movement styles. At one point a student would do a short movement motif cued by an artifact or by the weight, texture, mood, color, and the countless "cultural et ceteras" of the enveloping costume. Or, a student would assume a pose connoted by a costume, another student would "fit into" the design made by the first—and the generation of a motivated style was on its way. Stylistic movement patterns ensued. Among the most evocative patterns was one on the Greek kore, as well as an Arabic sequence inspired by a kaftan. An elongated, compelling design (suggested by a tubular jersey) was composed of two figures working contrapuntally. Totally encompassed by the style they were creating, the two were interdependent and laconic. Their nonverbalized inner action was so pervasive that an attempt at providing verbal instruction for physical action would have been an unnecessary intellectual exercise.

On another occasion, when lines of a poem were the starting point for a production, the sound of the words and their juxtaposition provided the springboard for the creation of movement style. Alternately angular, extravagant, and restrained, circular, the movement was punctuated by sudden brittle changes in rhythmicity which, nonetheless, seemed convincing in their authority. The audience's willingness to believe in the strange movement was the happy test of our procedures which had sought to involve the actors' human endowment and its needs within the invention of a style. And this goal is part of the synergy referred to earlier, the coherence which embraces also the requirements of the activity at hand and the demands posed by both the staged and the real environment.

It should go without saying that most theatre styles are best achieved by delving into the historical, authentic material.

Period and traditional movement and dance styles, in their actual patternings, are the obvious primary sources; and, as has been stated, our work makes use of this type of material.[9] Yet the purposes of this discussion can best be served by my providing illustrations of more unusual ways of working.

A favorite way involves the use of several collections of slides I've made. Reproductions and photos are assembled under the general headings of *Human Body Movement, The Human Condition* and *Styles in Art: What Do They Say of Styles in Movement?* Each of the assemblages comes into play at appropriate times.

The collection on art, for example, has been a particularly useful source of information on styles. Students begin with the pose and the activity depicted in bronze, stone, or paint by first ascertaining the inner physical action within the torso. (Is the inner action—to lie heavily, fully? To thrust the self sideward? To twist toward something? To reach? To give up in despair? To be molded by a corset?) After finding the type of energy which animates the torso and after exploring this perception physically, the details of the rest of the pose are scrutinized for what they tell of movement and style. The depiction of environment by the art work is no less informative in terms of suggestion for style. When the "living sculptures" made by the students—rather than being superficial imitations or dumb show—are sensitively realized, living moments, we go to the next stage. Now the aim is to find the movement which preceded as well as the movement that issues from the moment frozen by the original pose. Stylized movement results, often round and full, often jagged, intense; slow or fast, heavy, light, sometimes extended in range; usually expressive of the activity and of the environment portrayed by the work of art which prompted the whole experiment. The stylization has grown out of a valid physical experience, not out of mere imitativeness. Classic, familiar styles, remote styles, and newly created movement schemes that are the harvest of our careful nurturing have taught the actors procedures for finding style.

This is an indication, then, of how the approaches of our earlier work converge in the later developments. "What is the physical action inside what I am doing?" becomes "What is the physical action within the model?" As we try to arrive at the gist of a movement style, our explorations have encompassed Greek archaic and classical styles, medieval, renaissance, Shakespearean, restoration, nineteenth-century dramatists' styles, and also movement emanating from avant-garde approaches. The nearer we get to the experiential observance of the natural, the less the stylized, the selected, and the exaggerated present a polarity. The natural and the stylized become one embodiment.

FOOTNOTES

[1] F. Matthias Alexander, who practiced primarily in England, conceived the use of the head as "primary control" in the cultivation of favorable alignment. Although he had written four books, his work is better described by others, among them: Wilfred Barlow, *The Alexander Technique* (New York: Knopf, 1973); Edward Maisel, *The Resurrection of the Body,* (New York: University Books, 1969); Frank Pierce Jones, *Body Awareness in Action* (New York: Schocken Books, 1976); James H. Bierman, "The Alexander Technique 'Gets Its Directions,' " *Dance Scope* (Spring–] Summer 1978). Dr. Lulu Sweigard (who died in 1974, extended the discoveries of Mabel Todd and taught at the Juilliard School), *Human Movement Potential: Its Ideokinetic Facilitation* (New York: Dodd, Mead, 1973). Charlotte Selver is the definitive innovator-teacher of Sensory Awareness, whose work is best described in C. V. W. Brooks, *Sensory Awareness: the Rediscovery of Experiencing,* (New York: Viking, 1974). Also: Valentina Litvinoff, in her column, *A Round with Val,* "A Study in Consciousness," American Dance Guild *Newsletter* (March 1978). For a comparative discussion of the work of all three exponents (Sweigard, Alexander, and Selver), see Litvinoff, "Of Sweigard, Body Education, and Kindred Things," *Dance Scope* (Winter 1976).

[2] For a description of departures in dance movement from the original Method of Physical Action, see Litvinoff, *The Use of Stanislavsky Within Modern Dance* (New York: American Dance Guild, 1972).

[3] Fritz Popken presented a paper, "Efficiency in Movement Through Ideokinesis," as a member of a panel on Recent Research in Body Education, led by V. Litvinoff, at the Conference of the Committee on Research in Dance and the Society for Ethnomusicology, San Francisco, 1974.

[4] Nikolaas Tinbergen, "Ethology and Stress Diseases," *Science* (July 1974). Wilfred Barlow, M.D., *The Alexander Technique* (New York: Knopf, 1973).

[5] Pavel V. Simonov, "Methods of Physical Activities," *Interscaena* (Prague, July 1971).

[6] For examples of vital coordinations in movement; see Litvinoff, "Lessons From the Dancing Ground to the Studio: Implications of Pueblo Indian Dance for Modern Dance," *The Journal of Aesthetics and Art Criticism* (Spring 1974).

[7] Sophia Delza, "T'ai Chi Chuan," *The Drama Review* (March 1972).

[8] The series was brought from China to the Soviet Union under the aegis of the Russian medical organization and Medgis, the government publishers of medical literature. A paperback describing this version of T'ai Chi by Professor Gleb I. Krasnoselsky, who was one of the scientists and physiologists doing the original research on T'ai Chi in China, was published by Medgis in 1961. The physiologists, with health pursuits in mind, recommended this particular form for practice by the Russian people. And it is this series, which I was fortunate enough to obtain and study, that I teach. (I was glad to introduce a few of the series in the course of five days' sessions I conducted in 1973 as a seminar for the Theatre Movement Program of the American Theatre Association.)

[9] The use of ethnic and historical movement and dance styles has been discussed in Litvinoff, "How the Human Being Becomes an Instrument in the Theatre," *The Journal of Aesthetic Education* (July 1975). (Reprinted in *Exchange*, Spring 1976.)

Illustrations

Cover photograph by James Hay, Department of Bio-Mechanics, University of Iowa.

Drawings on page 3 by Aileen Crow.

Photographs on pages 19 and 20 by James Hay, Department of Bio-Mechanics, University of Iowa.

Drawings on pages 32, 35, 37, 40, 41, 43, and 46 by Patricia Relph.

Drawings on the title page (*ii*) and pages 57 and 59–67 by Linda Conaway.

Photographs on pages 75, 77, and 78 courtesy of Sears A. Eldredge and Hollis W. Huston.

Photograph on page 89 courtesy of Richard Nichols.

Photographs on pages 113 and 118 courtesy of Valentina Litvinoff.

Credits

Cover design by Elaine Golt Gongora.

Book design by Dennis J. Grastorf, The Angelica Studio.

Composition by Burmar Technical Corporation.

Printed by Noble Offset Printers, Inc.